WILLIAMS-SONOMA

Wine & Food

a new look at flavor

Joshua Wesson

GENERAL EDITOR	Chuck Williams
RECIPES	Coleen and Bob Simmons
PHOTOGRAPHS	Tucker + Hossler

GOLD STREET PRESS

Wine styles

Recipes

If you think of wine styles as expressions of flavor, pairing wine with food becomes a deliciously simple art.

About this book

I can vividly recall my first wine and food match. I was five years old, and it featured kosher wine made from Concord grapes paired with gefilte fish at our family Seder. It was a match with a clear message—Don't give Moses the corkscrew again!—but also one with a timeless wine-and-food lesson: trust your palate, rather than any rules etched in stone, and decide for yourself if the match is a good one. Forty years and thousands of bottles later, I can tell you that wisdom is every bit as sage. Of course, the old rules for selecting wine made life simple: white with fish, red with meat, and beer when in doubt. But today, most of us want to know the reasons behind the pairings we choose. This book serves that cause well. The good news is that the business—and pleasure—of wine and food pairing is grounded in common sense, requiring little more than a whiff of curiosity, and an attentive nose and tongue to get it right. In deference to that, I hope you enjoy the unique partnerships inside these pages. All are palate pleasing, and some, even a bit provocative. As provoking pleasure has become my life's pursuit, here's to doubling yours. Enjoy!

John A. Wesson

Wine fundamentals

The first wine may have come about when a Stone Age cave dweller left wild grapes in a tree hollow and forgot about them. In a few days, the grape juice fermented and turned into wine. The intoxicating beverage was served with the day's hunt, and the first food and wine pairing was born.

In truth, matching food and wine is a fairly recent concept. In the past, people simply served the local foods with whatever wine was available, especially in wine-producing areas. Fast forward hundreds of years and the teaming of good food with fine wine has become, in restaurants as well as some households, an art form.

Pairing the right wine with the right food creates something greater than the sum of the parts. But the idea that there is a perfect wine match for every food is inherently flawed, as a "good" wine and food pairing relies on the subjective opinions of the people who are eating and drinking. Throughout this book we will present many guidelines for what we think works and doesn't work, but in the end it is up to you to decide whether or not you enjoy a combination. But before we delve into food and wine pairing theories, it is helpful to ground yourself in a few basics about the world of wine.

The traditional grape-growing areas are centered in Europe and include Greece, France, Germany, Italy, and Spain, among others. These classic regions, with long histories of making fine wines, are often referred to in winespeak as the "Old World." During the last half century, wines from the newer regions of North and South America, Australia, New Zealand, and South Africa, have come into their own, frequently matching in quality many of the wines from the Old World wine regions. These modern wine-growing regions are referred to as the "New World." It is believed that New World winemakers tend to employ technology more than tradition to craft their wines.

In the Old World, and increasingly in the New, there is a tradition of tracing the grapes' qualities to the land on which they were grown. This sense of place is called the wine's *terroir*. This hard-to-define term refers to the influence that every aspect of a vineyard site—including soil, sun exposure, wind direction, microclimate, and any other natural element— has on the wine when it is brought together with human factors.

Old World

"Old World" refers to those countries where wine grapes were first widely planted, namely European regions. Old World techniques, by extension, refer to ways of growing grapes and making wines that rely as much on tradition as on technology. In general, Old World wines are subtle, complex, and heavily associated with place, be it a region, village, or vineyard.

New World

"New World" refers to all of the wine-producing countries that do not belong to the Old World, including the United States, Australia, New Zealand, South Africa, Argentina, and Chile. In general, New World wines utilize modern grape-growing and wine-making methods that rely heavily on technology. New World techniques can also refer to a style of wine typified by up-front flavor and fruit, a style that originated in California and then spread to other areas.

How wine is made

All wines, whether white or red, start as clear grape juice. The amount of time the juice comes in contact with grape skins determines the color of the finished wine. As we have mentioned, the grapes' *terroir* can have a strong influence on the flavor of wine. So, too, can each of the six steps involved in winemaking: picking, crushing, pressing, fermenting, maturing, and bottling.

White wine

After picking, the next step in making a still white wine involves crushing the grapes to break their skins. The grapes are pressed just after crushing to separate the juice from the skins. The juice is then fermented in stainless-steel or oak barrels, depending on the style of wine, followed by maturing—usually just for a short time—and then bottling.

Red wine

After crushing, red, or purple, grapes are fermented with their skins, which add color, tannin (an astringent substance that enables wine to age), and flavor to the wine. The grapes are then pressed to separate the juice from the skins, and before bottling, the young wine is matured in stainless steel tanks or oak barrels, depending on the style desired.

Rosé wine

Rosé starts just like red wine, but the fermenting juice is kept in contact with the skins for a much shorter time, often only a few hours. This process allows some color to be extracted from the grape skins, but very little tannin. Some sparkling rosés are made by blending a little red wine or fermenting red grape juice with still white wine.

Sparkling wine

The best sparkling wine starts as still wine, which is then fermented a second time. This secondary fermentation produces carbon dioxide, which, when trapped in the still wine, forms the bubbles. For sparkling wine to be called Champagne, it must be made from any or all of three different grape varieties (see page 36); the grapes must be grown in Champagne, France; and the wine must be produced using the Champagne method—a lengthy, labor-intensive, and expensive process in which the secondary fermentation takes place in the bottle in which the wine is sold.

Dessert wine and Port

For the great dessert wines, the grapes are left on the vine until the regular harvest has ended. This concentrates the natural sugars in the grapes. In certain fine wine regions, and in the best years, they may be affected by *botrytis cinerea,* or noble rot. This causes the skins to break, so much of the liquid in the grapes evaporates, concentrating the sugars further. Making Port involves the addition of neutral grape spirits to arrest the fermentation and preserve the natural grape sugar. It's then aged for varying amounts of time in barrels or bottles, depending on the preferred style.

Wine barrels

The type of barrel used to mature wine is critical. New oak barrels impart wood tannins to wine, while older oak barrels add softness and complexity. Oak barrels also expose the wine to small amounts of oxygen (the wood is permeable by air), which speeds up the maturation process. Barrel size is key, too. The bigger the barrel, the less effect it will have on the wine's flavor.

The bottle

Savvy wine drinkers know that certain iconic bottle shapes, as well as the color of the bottle glass, can give a clue about the wine style before you ever remove the cork.

Some of the characteristic bottle shapes shown here are associated with particular wine regions and can give information about the style of wine inside. While most of these bottle shapes originate in the Old World, New World producers will often use the representative bottle shape for wines of a similar style. The glass color, too, can reveal where a wine is from, hinting at its relative style, among other attributes.

In recent years, some producers, particularly in the New World, have abandoned the traditional shapes in favor of eye-catching bottles with wide, flanged mouths or other unusual features. When purchasing these, look to label cues or ask a knowledgeable friend or trusted wine merchant to help you judge the style of the wine.

Corks & other bottle closures

The bark of a type of oak tree, cork is the traditional closure for wine bottles. Recently, some producers have turned to alternative closures such as plastic corks or metal screw caps to both preserve the cork trees and eliminate the problem of cork taint, which affects about five percent of cork-sealed wines.

Champagne bottle

This bottle is constructed with a deep hollow in the bottom, called a "punt," which helps the glass withstand the immense pressure caused by trapped carbon dioxide. (For more on sparkling wines, turn to page 36).

White Bordeaux bottle

This clear, straight-sided bottle was first used for dry white Bordeaux. A wine in this type of bottle is likely a crisp or rich white (page 50 or 80). Pink wines (page 96) and sweet wines (page 154) can also be found in this shape.

Alsace or Riesling bottle

Pale green or brown, this slender bottle is used for white wines from Northern France and Germany. If you see a wine in this style of bottle, it probably will be a soft white (page 66).

Burgundy bottle

This bottle, with its sloping sides, features yellow or green glass. A white wine in a yellow bottle probably means a rich white (page 80). A red wine in a green bottle will be a juicy or smooth red (page 110 or 124).

Red Bordeaux bottle

This green-cast bottle is almost universally used for Cabernet Sauvignon, Merlot, and Bordeaux-style blends. This bottle usually signifies that a wine is a smooth or bold red (page 124 or 140).

Port bottle

Made from very dark green or almost black glass, this distinctive squat bottle, made specifically for Port, is easily recognized by its slightly bulging neck. (For more on Port, turn to page 154.)

The label

There are different conventions for New World and Old World wine labels. Knowing the differences can give clues about wine styles and help guide your choice at the wine shop.

There are four key pieces of information to look for on the wine label: Where the wine was made; the variety of grapes that was used; the name of the producer; and the year the grapes were harvested. This information is conveyed differently from country to country, even region to region.

In general, New World wine labels categorize their wines by grape varietal, whereas Old World wines call out the region in which the grapes were grown, which, by extension, reveals what types of grapes are used to make the wine. New World wine labels have little to denote quality standards, other than the reputation of the producer. Old-World wines, on the other hand, often include a governmentally regulated stamp of quality.

Misleading labels

From time to time, you may find words or phrases on U.S. wine labels that attempt to give the wine a quality aura. But words such as "Proprietor's Reserve" and "Cellar Selection" have no legal definition. Instead of relying on these vague descriptions, get to know the wines on their own merits, or ask a trusted wine merchant for guidance.

U.S. wine label

On U.S. wine labels, as well as those of most other New World wines, the producer, followed by the grape varietal, is the main way in which wines are distinguished from one another. Some wine labels also indicate the district in which the wine was made, based on a system of American Viticultural Areas (AVAs), or a specific vineyard or vineyards, both of which can be an indication of quality.

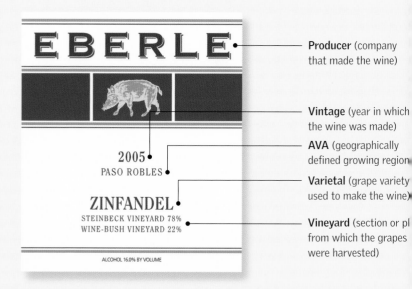

Producer (company that made the wine)

Vintage (year in which the wine was made)

AVA (geographically defined growing region)

Varietal (grape variety used to make the wine)

Vineyard (section or pl from which the grapes were harvested)

French wine label

A French wine label tends to focus on where the wine comes from. To determine what type of grapes and/or the style of wine in the bottle, it's helpful to have a working knowledge of the main wine regions and their customary grapes. French wine labels also have a number of quality classifications, which vary by region. A respected wine merchant can help you decipher confusing labels.

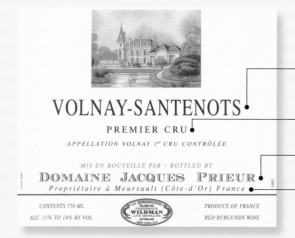

Wine region (geographically defined growing region)

Quality rank (based on regional standards)

Producer (wine house that made the wine)

Additional information (general wine region an district)

South American wine label

South America has borrowed its labeling customs from the United States wine industry, which has a longer-standing history of producing quality wines. In Argentina, Chile, and other countries, the wines are identified primarily by producer and varietal, with some geographical information linking the grapes to particular growing regions. As in the United States, the grapes are not necessarily tied to specific regions.

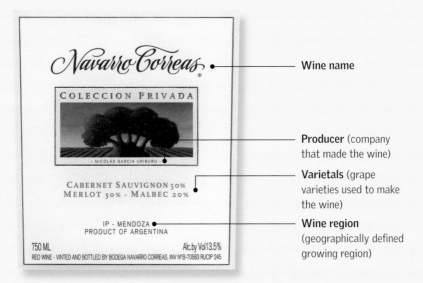

Wine name

Producer (company that made the wine)

Varietals (grape varieties used to make the wine)

Wine region (geographically defined growing region)

German wine label

German wine labels list information about the varietal and vintage as well as information about the ripeness of grapes and the quality standards of the wine. These labels may seem confusing at first, but once you learn to recognize a few key terms and what they mean, you'll be able to pick out the perfect German wine for the occasion. See pages 68 and 156 for more information on German wines.

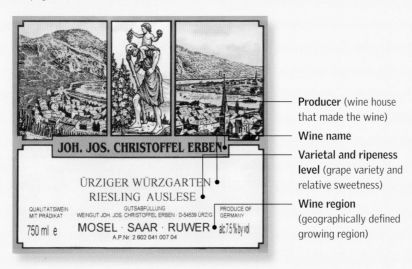

Producer (wine house that made the wine)

Wine name

Varietal and ripeness level (grape variety and relative sweetness)

Wine region (geographically defined growing region)

Regional information

Originating from the French notion that the sense of place is a critical factor in crafting a wine, many New World wine-makers list a place of origin, or *appellation,* on their labels. In general, the more specific the region, the higher quality the wine. For example, a wine labeled simply "Sonoma County" can use grapes from throughout Sonoma. But a wine labeled "Dry Creek" means that the grapes can only come from that small, defined area of the county, implying more control over production, and hence a better wine.

Opening wine

Uncorking a bottle of still or sparkling wine might seem tricky, but the best way to get familiar with the process is simply to open a lot of bottles. Use the following methods as a guide.

There is a wide, perhaps even confusing, selection of corkscrews on the market. The choice really depends on what style is easiest for you to use. Most professionals (and many amateurs) prefer a simple corkscrew called the "waiter's friend," which uses leverage to extract the cork.

The most important element of the corkscrew is the wire spiral, or worm. It should be at least 2 inches long, so that it will penetrate deep enough into the cork to remove it without breaking or otherwise damaging it. Look for a round worm with a sharp point and an open spiral that will firmly grip the cork. Avoid winged corkscrews, whose screw-like tips bore a hole into the cork, particularly dry ones, pushing cork bits into the wine as you open it.

Other wine openers
The Ah-So wine opener, consisting of two flat metal blades attached to an oval handle, is a cult favorite for some aficionados. The thin blades are inserted between the cork and the bottle, then the cork is twisted out. A lever pull opener has a clever clamp-and-lever system, which neatly opens wine using an extra-long, Teflon-coated worm.

Opening still wine

Although screw caps are becoming more widely used, most wines are still packaged with a natural or synthetic cork, which must be removed using a wine opener. A waiter's corkscrew is an efficient tool for opening wine, as its foldaway knife can also remove the foil or wax cap on the top of most wine bottles. In addition, the wine opener's slim line makes it easy to store.

Opening sparkling wine

Opening a bottle of sparkling wine makes some people nervous, as the sudden release of pressure can emit a loud noise and cause the wine to overflow. Follow the steps outlined here and you'll be able to control the speed at which the cork is released—with a hiss, rather than a pop—and keep all the wine where it should be—in the glass.

1 Trim the foil cap
Open the corkscrew's blade and align the blade along the bottle's top or bottom lip. Press the blade firmly as you rotate the bottle with your other hand. Pull off the foil cap, exposing the cork.

1 Chill the wine
Thoroughly chilled sparkling wine is much less likely to pop unexpectedly when you open it. If the wine has not already been chilled, place it in an ice bucket filled with ice and water for about 20 minutes.

2 Insert the corkscrew

Pull out the corkscrew's lever, then open the spiral worm so that it is fully exposed. Align the point of the worm in the center of the cork, then twist the worm straight down into the cork.

3 Extract the cork

Fold in the lever and place it on the rim of the bottle. Place your other hand around the bottle and hold the lever firmly. Pull up on the handle of the corkscrew to slowly remove the cork.

4 Pour the wine

Wipe the lip of the bottle with a towel, then evaluate the wine (see page 24). Pour a glass, filling it one-third to one-half full. Twist your wrist slightly at the end to prevent drips.

2 Remove the wire cage

Peel off the foil covering from the top of the bottle, then twist open and remove the wire cage, keeping one hand firmly on top of the cork. This will prevent the cork from popping out before you are ready.

3 Ease out the cork

Hold the bottle at a 45-degree angle. Cover the cork with a dish towel and grip it tightly. With your other hand, slowly twist the bottle—not the cork. The cork should slowly slide out with just a faint popping noise.

4 Pour the wine

Holding the bottle by the base, pour the sparkling wine into flutes, filling each glass only about halfway to prevent overflow. As the bubbles subside, go back and top off the glasses, filling them about three-quarters full.

The glass

A tumbler of rustic wine makes a simple, casual statement. But there are times when the occasion or the wine demand a stemmed wine glass. Here's a primer on what's available.

A good set of basic wine glasses will not only add flair to your table, but can also enhance the flavor of the wine. Dozens of different shapes are available—specialists have developed forms for most of the major wine varieties and regions, even specific vintages. But all you really need are two basic shapes: flutes, for sparkling wines, and tulip-shaped glasses for still wines. If you like to serve two types of still wine at a meal, consider buying two sets of tulip glasses: a smaller glass for white wine and a larger glass for red wine.

As your tastes expand, or your wine budget grows, you can add specialized shapes, such as those shown here, or higher-quality stemware. But no matter what type of glass you purchase, always choose glassware made of clear glass with thin rims.

Wine decanters

Wines are sometimes decanted before serving to aerate them and smooth out their tannins (young wines) or to remove sediment (old wines) with the aid of a light source. If purchasing a decanter, as with wine glasses, choose one that is made of clear glass and is lightweight enough to pass around the table. A stopper is optional.

Flute
The narrow shape of this glass, used for sparkling wines, preserves the wine's bubbles and directs them vertically up the glass.

Small tulip glass
This all-purpose glass has plenty of room in the bowl to swirl the wine and sample the wine's aromas, which are concentrated around the rim of the glass.

Large tulip glass
A red wine's bouquet is usually more developed tha that of white wine. This gla has a bigger bowl, which helps you swirl fine red win more efficiently.

Riesling glass

The slightly curved lip of this glass directs the flow of wine to the tip of the tongue, the area where the perception of sweetness is the greatest. This accentuates the fruit and tempers the acidity, which works well for soft or crisp white wines.

Burgundy glass

Red Burgundies and new-world Pinot Noirs release their aromas very quickly. The wider bowl and tapering sides of the Burgundy glass have been designed to maximize these aromas.

Bordeaux glass

This large glass, with its gently tapering sides, provides maximum contact with the air, allowing the aroma and flavor of red Bordeaux and similar wines to develop.

Port glass

Port is traditionally served in small quantities. This slim, tapering glass allows you to serve the correct quantity of wine while allowing room in the bowl to swirl the wine and appreciate Port's complex bouquet. This glass is also suitable for a variety of sweet wines.

Evaluating wine

Evaluating wine involves four steps—looking, swirling, sniffing, and sipping. Each step gives you key information about the wine, and can also inform what food to serve with it.

Tasting a wine begins with the eyes. Just looking at a wine can tell you a lot about what to expect. For example, wines from hot climates generally have a deeper color than wines from cool climates. Older wines usually have a less intense color than young wines. But looking is, of course, not the only way to judge a wine. Swirling, smelling, and, finally, tasting the wine can confirm or contradict what you perceived from the appearance.

Your sense of smell plays a more important part in your perception of a wine than your sense of taste, which is actually fairly limited. Professional wine critics have a special vocabulary for wine aromas and flavors. Don't worry if you don't detect these same smells and flavors; what's most important is how the wine smells and tastes to you.

Wine faults

Tainted wine is rare these days, but there are still some common faults to look out for. "Corked" wine is caused by a mold in cork bark that gives the wine an off flavor. Oxidized wine has been exposed too long to air, giving it a dull brown color and sour flavor. Vinegary wine has been affected by a bacteria, rendering it unpleasantly sharp.

1 Look

Hold the glass by its stem in order to keep the bowl free of smudges and handprints. Hold the glass against a white background, such as a napkin or a clean piece of paper and peer at the wine—this will give you a true idea of the wine's clarity and color. The appearance will vary, but in general, a white wine should be transparent and bright, and a red wine should be translucent and brilliant.

2 Swirl

Next, holding the stem of the glass, swirl the wine carefully. This introduces oxygen into the wine, which helps release its essential aromas. In some wines, you may notice distinct tracks left on the inside of the glass, called "legs," which are caused by the alcohol in the wine. Wines with a high alcohol content will show pronounced legs that linger on the side of the glass. Wines with a low percentage of alcohol will show faint legs that dissipate quickly.

3 Sniff

Now, put your nose over the rim of the glass and inhale long and deep through your nose. Really expand your nostrils to take in the smell. Try to think what memory you associate with the smell (the olfactory memories are some of the strongest we have). You may want to repeat this process several times. Younger wines usually have stronger, more aggressive aromas, while older wines are generally more subdued, subtle, and complex.

AROMA & BOUQUET These two terms are sometimes used interchangeably, but technically each has a different meaning. Aroma refers to the smell of a young wine, or of the grapes used to make the wine. As the wine matures, and the scents become more complex, the aroma changes to bouquet.

4 Sip

Finally, fill your mouth about one-third full and swish the wine around thoroughly. This causes more aromas to be released into the nasal cavity, which is where the real "tasting" happens. It also helps the wine to reach all parts of your palate to gain a complete impression of the wine. Some people describe this process as "chewing" the wine. As you swallow, pay attention to how the wine feels in the mouth, how the taste changes as the wine slips down your throat, and how long the wine's flavor lingers on your tongue.

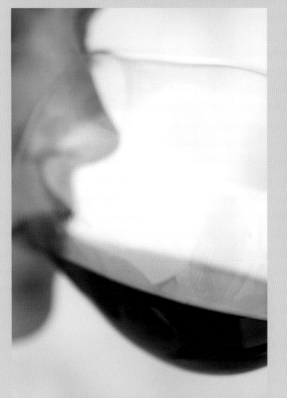

BODY A wine's body is the feeling of substance it forms in the mouth, described in terms of weight, fullness, or texture. Body, or mouthfeel, can be understood on a spectrum from skim milk (a light-bodied wine) to heavy cream (a full-bodied wine).

FINISH The length of time the wine's aftertaste lingers on the tongue is called its finish. Wines with lingering aftertastes, or long finishes, are often thought to be of better quality than those with little or no finish, but in truth, it will depend on the style of wine that you are drinking.

Sensual perceptions in wine & food

In the past, local foods were served with whatever wine was available. But over the years, as wine and food traditions globalized, there has been a growing interest in wine and food pairing. As you evaluate the wine (page 24), pay attention to the aromas, tastes, and textures that you perceive. Becoming familiar with these building blocks is the first step in learning to create a great food and wine match.

Aromatic elements

Smelling wine reveals a range of scents that distinguish them. Perceived by the olfactory system, these flavor perceptions include such descriptions as "grassy," "nutty," or "floral," among dozens of others. It is in this category that you find people waxing poetic about what they can smell in wine, but these perceptions are highly subjective. For example, one person's "freshly mown lawn" could be another's "just-picked asparagus"; one person's "barnyard" might be someone else's "leather saddle." Despite their debate-sparking tendencies, these flavors figure prominently in creating a wine-food match.

Throughout the book, we offer a "flavor profile" for each wine style, which presents a snapshot of the common aromatic, taste, and tactile elements found in each type of wine. These profiles will give you a sense of what to expect, but remember that specific wines will have unique attributes and will be interpreted in various ways by different people.

Taste elements

Tasting wine and food reveals a set of perceptions that can only be perceived by the tongue. In wine, the three main taste elements are sweetness, acidity, and bitterness. In food, saltiness and hot-spiciness are also part of the picture. Being able to perceive the taste elements is perhaps the most important factor in determining the success of a food and wine match. If one or more taste elements is pronounced, it is likely the most important element to consider when creating the pairing.

Unlike the aromatic elements, the taste elements are measurable. For example, it is possible to detect how much residual sugar is present in a wine, or whether the wine is high or low in acidity. Therefore, pairings based on taste elements can be somewhat more objective than that of aromatic elements. As you taste each wine and imagine food you might pair with it, think about the taste elements you perceive: The interplay of sweet, sour, bitter, salty, and hot-spicy all play a part in a good wine and food match.

Pairing aromas

Serving wines with foods that have similar aromas is a smart strategy. You can also use herbs, fruits, nuts and other flavorful companion ingredients to help reinforce a similar scent in a wine. But because the perception of smells is subjective, use your judgment when pairing aromas with dissimilar flavors. For example, does "smoky" matched with "floral" seem appealing? Perhaps "cheesy" combined with "nutty"? Pairings based on aromatic elements are attractive only when they are appealing to you.

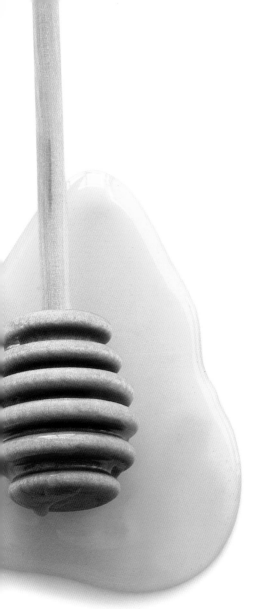

ACIDITY A natural component of grapes, acidity, or tartness, helps the wine achieve balance and structure. As you taste the wine, try to discern the level of acidity present. A wine with too much acidity will taste unpleasantly sharp. A wine with too little acidity can taste dull and flat. Sourness is also an important component in food. Dishes prepared with vinegar, lemon juice, or some fruits are highly acidic and can present a challenge when matching them to wine.

BITTERNESS The bitter factor in wine comes from grape skins and from substances found in oak barrels. Bitterness is more common in red wines than in white, but you sometimes find a hint of it in hot-climate, oak-aged white wines. Bitterness is an important component of food as well. Artichokes, some leafy greens, and cruciferous vegetables are examples of bitter foods. Cooking methods that involve charring or searing can also add bitter flavors to the dish.

SWEETNESS Wines are categorized on a spectrum of dry to sweet, based on the level of residual sugar left in the wine after fermentation. When you taste the wine, note the level of sugar that you detect in your mouth. A "dry" wine refers to a wine with no perceivable sweetness. Food, too, can have sweet components, but it doesn't always mean sugar has been added. For example, fruits, vegetables, and aged balsamic vinegar all provide a measure of sweetness to a recipe. You can also add sweetness to a dish by searing or caramelizing the ingredients, which bring out the food's natural sugars.

SALTINESS Wine typically does not have salty flavors, but saltiness is still an important consideration in pairing wine and food. In food, saltiness comes from natural salt—think of briny shellfish—or salt added to a recipe. The saltier a dish, the more limited you are in matching it to wine. But don't let that dissuade you from using salt in a recipe. Often just the right amount of it can bring out the best in a dish, helping it match better to any wine.

SPICINESS In wine, what is considered "spicy" actually refers to the impression of a spice like pepper or anise, which is perceived through the nose as an aromatic element. Here, we are referring to the "hot" sensation contributed by chile peppers, which is present in a variety of foods and can be a challenge to match to wine. Used in excess, chiles can numb the palate or make the wine's individual elements seem stronger or out of balance.

Pairing tastes

Matching wine and food with similar taste elements often works well. For example, tart foods taste best paired with acidic wines. Sweet foods stand up well to sweet wine, as long as the wine that's chosen is sweeter than the food. Some bitter foods, like char-grilled steaks, are wonderful with bitter, tannic red wines. Pairing dissimilar taste elements can also work well: salty foods are nicely offset by acidic and slightly sweet wines. Moderately spicy foods are tempered by acidic or off-dry wines.

Tactile elements

Also known as the "texture" of wine and food, tactile elements relate to the sensation of touch. You've already read about a wine's body, or how it feels in the mouth (see page 25). Related to body is the wine's alcohol content, which registers as both heft and warmth on the palate. Wines that are high in alcohol can be described as "heavy" and "hot." Lower-alcohol wines feel lighter and cooler in the mouth. Another important textural element of wine is tannin, an astringent substance that comes from both grape skins and oak barrels. Tannin causes a dry, puckery sensation on the tongue and sides of the mouth, like sipping a cup of overbrewed tea. Food presents more textural properties on which to base a match: A dish can be dense or loose, grainy or smooth, hot or cold.

Layering elements

The best wine and food matches occur when the aromatic, taste, and tactile elements come together in harmony. But one element—frequently a taste element—will probably stand out as most prominent. When creating your own pairings, focus on the most striking element as a starting point. As you become more confident in your matching skills, you'll be able to incorporate additional elements to create even more appealing pairings. Turn to page 30 to learn how to get started.

Pairing textures

Coupling wine and food with similar body is a wise choice. Light wines are the perfect match for light food, which would be overwhelmed by a full-bodied wine. Bold wines go well with rich foods, provided the pairing isn't too heavy overall. When pairing dissimilar textures, take care: Pair rich food with light wine or light food with rich wine only if the bolder partner doesn't overwhelm the less assertive partner. Consider temperature, too, when creating a match based on texture. Warm food and cold wine can be a wonderful, refreshing combination.

Creating a wine & food match

As you have seen, great wine and food pairings are based on emphasizing the similarities or highlighting the differences in the sensual perceptions of both the wine and food. In wine, the elements are predetermined. But in a recipe, a match can be facilitated by choosing appropriate main ingredients, companion ingredients, and cooking methods that complement or contrast with the chosen style of wine.

Difficult ingredients

Old wine-and-food-pairing rules discouraged people from using certain ingredients in recipes, as the interplay of the food and the wine will change the flavors adversely. Artichokes, asparagus, chocolate, eggs, and salads are common culprits. However, if you prepare the ingredients with care, add the right companion ingredients, and pair them with a suitable wine, any ingredient can work well with wine. You'll find many such examples throughout the book.

Main ingredient

The main ingredient refers to the item that forms the central focus of the dish, be it meat, poultry, fish, shellfish, or vegetables. Many people use the main recipe ingredient as the basis for creating a food and wine match, particularly those who are just learning about wine and food pairing. It is through the complement or contrast of the main ingredient that the conventional rules of food and wine pairing have come about. For example, white wine has traditionally been matched with fish in part because its tactile elements—light food and light wine—are complementary. Heavy red meats have historically been paired with full-bodied red wines for the same reason.

Companion ingredients

Often the main ingredient serves as a neutral backdrop for powerful seasonings and sauces; in these instances the companion ingredients are perhaps more important than the main ingredient in creating the wine match. Companion ingredients include cooking fats, sauces or relishes, or specific ingredients— mushrooms, spices, or herbs—that have a special affinity with a particular wine. For

example, lamb chops, based solely on color and texture, call for a red wine with medium to full body. Add a rosemary-based marinade, and suddenly a Cabernet Sauvignon springs to mind. The rosemary helps form a stronger link with the herb-scented wine than if the recipe did not feature rosemary. In other words, the secondary ingredient forms a complement with the wine's aromatic elements. Wine itself can become a companion ingredient in a recipe and help reinforce a match. Simply add a little of the wine you plan to drink, or one that's similar, to a sauce or braising liquid.

Cooking methods

The cooking method can also contribute aromas, tastes, or textures to the food, and hence figure prominently in the wine match. For example, charcoal-grilled foods are good companions for wines with pronounced oak flavors, a match formed by complementing the smoky elements in each partner. Caramelizing vegetables brings out their natural sugars, which can help them match better to off-dry wines. Braising adds weight and richness to foods, which helps them form a stronger link to fuller-bodied wine styles.

Using the flavor profiles

To guide you in pairing wine with food, the book is organized around nine "flavor profiles," which group the wines around common elements. These include: Sparkling Wines (page 35); Crisp Whites (page 49); Soft Whites (page 65); Rich Whites (page 79); Pink Wines (page 95); Juicy Reds (page 109); Smooth Reds (page 123); Bold Reds (page 139); and Sweet Wines (page 153). The chart that follows lists main and companion ingredients and cooking methods that, when combined, form classic food-and-wine pairings within their respective styles. Turn to the individual chapters for detailed information.

	Sparkling Wines	Crisp Whites	Soft Whites	Rich Whites
Main ingredients	caviar mollusks crustaceans fish smoked fish mild poultry smoked poultry eggs mild meats	mollusks crustaceans mild white fish smoked salmon mild poultry mild meats	mollusks crustaceans mild white fish meaty fish poultry game birds charcuterie smoked meats pork	mollusks crustaceans fish poultry game birds mild meats
Companion ingredients	butter & cream chiles citrus nuts soy sauce aged cheeses double- & triple cream cheeses	butter chiles & garlic citrus fruits fresh herbs green vegetables mild vinegar olives & capers tomatoes goat & sheep cheese	chiles citrus fruits coconut milk exotic spices fresh herbs soy & fish sauce tree fruits washed-rind cheeses	avocados butter & cream corn & mushrooms exotic spices fresh herbs garlic mustard nuts tree fruits cow's milk cheeses
Cooking methods	deep-frying poaching sautéing	grilling poaching sautéing	braising grilling steaming	braising grilling roasting

Putting it all together

As you work your way through the book, you will begin to see how we created the recipes using the formula outlined in pages 26–33. When you're ready, you'll be able to use this same thinking to construct perfect pairings of your own. The chart below can be used as a starting point to put together a dish with a specific wine style in mind. Or, you can use the chart to help find a wine style that matches a particular dish featuring the listed elements. Above all, remember that the information in the book is just a guideline, a starting point. Only you can decide if the food and wine match is true magic.

Pink Wines	Juicy Reds	Smooth Reds	Bold Reds	Sweet Wines
mollusks	meaty fish	meaty fish	dark-meat poultry	chocolate
meaty fish	poultry	poultry	game birds	custards
poultry	game birds	game birds	strong sausages	cakes
game birds	charcuterie	sausage	marbled red meats	berries
smoked meats	sausage	pork & veal	game meats	tree fruits
charcuterie	pork & veal	lean red meats		puff & filo pastry
sausage	smoked meats	game meats		foie gras
pork	mild red meats			strong blue cheese
bold spices	cherries & berries	butter & cream	berries & plums	butter & cream
chiles & garlic	fresh herbs	cherries & berries	black pepper	caramel
citrus fruits	garlic	garlic	butter & cream	dried fruit
exotic spices	legumes	mushrooms	garlic	honey
fresh herbs	mushrooms	mustard	mushrooms	nuts
mushrooms	mustard	truffles	mustard	sugar
olives & capers	sweet spices	woody herbs	truffles	sweet spices
tomatoes	tomatoes		woody herbs	
		aged cow's milk cheeses		
mild or strong cheeses	aged or strong cheeses		aged hard cheeses	
			blue cheese	
deep-frying	braising	braising	braising	baking
grilling	grilling	roasting	grilling	poaching
sautéing	roasting	sautéing	roasting	roasting

Sparkling wines

Fizzy, yeasty, and mouthwatering, sparkling wines come in a collection of styles. Their light effervescence marries well with both special-occasion and casual fare.

From celebratory repasts to everyday meals, sparkling wines are a surprisingly versatile partner. They are popular aperitifs, thanks to their appetite-stimulating bubbles and tingling acid. But these qualities also make sparklers the perfect match for a wide variety of foods, from hors d'oeuvres to eggs to fish and poultry dishes. Winemakers throughout the globe emulate Champagne's traditional style with excellent results. But not everyone aims for the sophisticated nutty-creamy style of true Champagne. There are many fine examples of fruity, accessible sparkling wines, which go equally well—perhaps even better— with food, throughout the Old and New Worlds.

About sparkling wines

Sparkling wines are traditional companions for celebratory toasts and lavish hors d'oeuvres. But like crisp whites (page 49), sparkling wines boast high acidity, which helps them match a range of ingredients beyond what you would normally find on a tray of canapés. The bubbles, too, can create interesting textural pairings that are not possible with other styles of wine.

The Champagne method

Many of the world's quality sparkling wine producers employ a secondary fermentation of the wine in the bottle in which it is sold. On wine labels in Europe, the process is referred to as the traditional method. "Crémant" is another word used to describe wines made by the Champagne method outside of the region. Lesser-quality sparkling wines may employ a secondary fermentation technique that takes place in a tank, rather than in individual bottles.

Attributes of sparkling wines

Only sparkling wines that come from the Champagne region in northeastern France can legally be called Champagne in Europe. Some low-end American producers have borrowed the name, but most winemakers favor labeling their wines as *"méthode champenoise"* or "traditional method" to indicate that the wines are made from the historic trio of grapes (see page 38) and/or with Champagne's time-honored method of fermentation.

The acidity and effervescence of sparkling wines helps stimulate the appetite, making them perfect sipping wines. Sparkling wines are traditionally paired with luxury foods such as caviar, oysters, and foie gras, where their flavors and textures—and sometimes price tags—are a natural match. But sparkling wines are also surprisingly good with more casual fare, such as salty, deep-fried snacks. Here, the wine's acid tames the salt while at the same time it cuts through the richness of the food's cooking oil. Texturally, the match also works: the wine's crisp bubbles are perfectly suited to the crispness of a potato chip or fried wonton. Rich foods can also be apt companions for sparkling wines, whose acidity and effervescence do double duty to counteract fat. The unique combination of flavor and texture makes sparkling wine one of the few wines that can pair well with egg dishes, making it a perfect brunch beverage.

1 Look

The color of sparkling wines can range from very pale to straw to golden. New World wines can appear darker in color, as is typical in warmer-climate wines. Blanc de Noirs and sparkling rosés range in color from light salmon to deep pink.

2 Swirl

Sparkling wines do not need to be swirled, as their effervescence will cause the aromas to rise in the glass. Instead, take a moment to admire the bubbles. Legend has it that the smaller the bubbles, the finer the sparkling wine. In a quality wine, very small bubbles will rise in a constant stream.

3 Smell

The bubbles in sparkling wines will tickle your nose while releasing an enticing array of aromas. They're more likely to be yeasty and nutty in a Champagne or Champagne-style wine, and fruity and creamy in a New World wine or a sparkling wine made from a single grape varietal.

4 Sip

The first impression will be the palate-cleansing action of the bubbles, followed by the wine's tangy acid. Good sparklers have a nice balance of fruit, acidity, and soft effervescence, with a moderately long finish.

Flavor profile

Champagne is famous for its rich, toasty, and yeasty bouquet, which Old and New World producers alike try to emulate. A second camp makes sparkling wines with more pronounced fruit flavors and less complex structures in both the Old and New worlds. The latter tends to be more accessible to the everyday wine drinker and more universally suited to a wide range of foods.

Floral

This aroma is more often found in the less complex sparkling wines, or wines made from naturally floral grapes.

Dried cherry

A scent reminiscent of dried cherries is typical in Champagne-style wines and Blanc de Noirs, both of which feature cherry-scented Pinot Noir grapes.

Lemon

A lemony aroma and flavor comes from a wine's citric acid, which helps give it balance. It is found most often in cool-climate white wines.

Green apple

An aroma and flavor of green apples comes from the natural malic acid present in both grapes and apples.

Toast

A wine with a toasty aroma is common in Champagne and Champagne-style wines.

Mineral

A minerally aroma and flavor reflects the wine's *terrior*. Some claim they can actually taste the minerals from the soil in which the grapes were grown.

Pear

Some sparkling wines feature fruit aromas that are slightly softer and honeyed, more like pears than apples.

Hazelnut

The nutty flavor in many sparkling wines comes from the extensive aging of the wines.

Cream

A creamy wine refers to the mouth-filling impression left by a sparkling wine's froth, typical in wines featuring Chardonnay as well as some sparkling rosés.

Yeast

This tasting term refers to the fresh-baked-bread smell common in many sparkling wines, which comes from the traditional fermentation process.

Key sparkling wines

Most of the sparkling wine on the U.S. market is considered Brut (right), which denotes a relatively dry, food-friendly wine. In addition, most sparkling wines available in this country are "nonvintage" wines, meaning they are blended from grapes harvested over two or more years. This practice creates flavors and prices that are relatively consistent year after year.

Riddling & disgorging

After initial fermentation, Champagne is *riddled,* meaning the bottles are stacked in special racks and gently turned over a period of time. This process causes the sediment to move into the neck of the bottle. Next, the bottles are *disgorged,* which involves freezing the sediment in the bottle's neck, then popping off the temporary bottle cap. The trapped carbon dioxide gas propels the frozen sediment from the bottle. A mixture of wine and sugar syrup, called *dosage,* is added to the wine before corking; the *dosage* determines its final level of sweetness.

Champagne

Hailing from northern France, Champagne is the world's model for sparkling wine. By law, the wine can only be made from three grapes, one white and two red: Chardonnay lends elegance and green apple and citrus aromas; Pinot Noir adds complexity and red fruit flavors; and Pinot Meunier provides body and additional flavors to round out the blend. To be called Champagne, the wine must also employ the authentic method of fermentation (see page 36). Champagne comes in two main styles: vintage Champagne, made only in the best years from grapes of a single vintage; and nonvintage Champagne, made by blending wines from several years.

Sekt

A German sparkling wine, Sekt is made from Riesling, Pinot Blanc, and/or Pinot Gris grapes and employs the Champagne method of fermentation. Look for the word "trocken" on the label to indicate a dry wine.

Champagne-style sparkling wines

The United States, California in particular, produces high-quality sparkling wines using the traditional grapes (Chardonnay, Pinot Noir, and Pinot Meunier) and the traditional method (fermentation in the bottle), which rival those of their French cousins. Australia, Tasmania in particular; New Zealand; and South Africa also make delicious Champagne-inspired wines.

Crémant

This term refers to Champagne-method sparkling wine made outside the Champagne district. Some of the best come from Alsace, Burgundy, and the Loire. Crémant d'Alsace can be made from Pinot Blanc, Pinot Noir, Riesling, or other local grapes. Crémant d'Bourgogne is made from the Burgundian grapes Chardonnay and Pinot Noir. Crémant de Loire is a light, fruity blend of local grapes. Because they do not carry the Champagne name, but are nevertheless good-quality wines, Crémants can be good values.

Blanc de Blancs

The name, literally "white from whites," refers to the fact that this sparkling wine is made only from white Chardonnay grapes. Made in France and the United States, Blanc de Blancs tends to be lighter in body and somewhat creamier in style than traditional Champagne, with few of its toasty, nutty aromas.

Blanc de Noirs

Literally "white from blacks," the name of this sparkling wine reflects the use of only red-skinned grapes in the wine, customarily Pinot Noir and Pinot Meunier. The finished wine may have a slightly pink or salmon-colored hue. Made in France and in the U.S., Blanc de Noirs tends to be more full-bodied than other types of sparkling wine.

Sparkling Rosé

Sparkling rosé is taken very seriously in Europe, particularly France and Spain. The best are made from still pink wines, which are fermented a second time in the bottle. For more on rosés, turn to page 95.

Prosecco

Prosecco refers to the grape and the wine, made in the Veneto region of Italy. Gaining recently in popularity, this wine has a lovely "fruit salad" bouquet and light body. With none of the toasty-yeasty aromas common in a true Champagne, Prosecco is a verstile, high-acid partner for a variety of foods.

Cava

This Spanish sparkling wine uses the classical fermentation-in-the-bottle method made famous by Champagne, but instead uses grapes native to the region, including Macabeo, Parellada, and Xarel-lo. Chardonnay is also sometimes used for additional flavor and structure. Some believe Cava, with its similar yeasty aromas, to be just as good as Champagne, but it is usually much lower in price. Cavas can also be found as rosés.

Sparkling Vouvray

This elegant sparkling wine is made in the Loire valley from the Chenin Blanc grape. Look for the word *mousseux,* which is French for sparkling. It comes both dry and sweet.

Levels of sweetness in Champagne

True Champagne is made in a variety of sweetness levels, categorized as follows: *Extra* or *Ultra Brut* wines have either zero or minimal *dosage,* and taste very dry. These can be hard to find. *Brut* Champagne has less than 1.5 grams of sugar per liter added before bottling and is the most common type on the market. *Extra Dry* is a misleading term, as the residual sugar may be up to 6 percent and the wine tastes very sweet. *Demi-Sec, Sec,* and *Doux* are fully sweet versions and are the best types to pair with dessert.

Pork & shrimp wontons

The bubbles and acid in the wine team up to counteract the oily and salty elements of these deep-fried treats. The wine also forms an appealing contrast to the sweet-spicy dipping sauce.

2 dried shiitake mushrooms

1/2 lb ground pork

5 tbsp soy sauce

2 tsp Shaoxing wine or dry sherry

2 tsp cornstarch

2 tsp canola oil, plus more for frying

2 oz shrimp, peeled, deveined, and finely chopped

6 water chestnuts, finely chopped

4 green onions, finely chopped

1 tsp peeled and finely chopped fresh ginger

1 tsp Asian sesame oil

1 egg white

1/2 tsp kosher salt

Generous dash of ground white pepper

1 package (1 lb) square wonton wrappers

2/3 cup Thai sweet chile sauce

In a small bowl, soften the mushrooms in hot water for 10–15 minutes. Meanwhile, in a bowl, mix together the pork, 1 tablespoon of the soy sauce, the wine, and the cornstarch. In a frying pan over medium heat, warm the 2 teaspoons canola oil. Add the pork mixture and cook, stirring, until it is no longer pink, 4–5 minutes. Using a slotted spoon, transfer the pork mixture to a clean bowl. Drain the mushrooms, squeeze dry, and discard the stems. Chop the mushrooms into 1/4-inch pieces and add to the bowl with the pork mixture. Add the shrimp, water chestnuts, green onions, ginger, sesame oil, egg white, salt, and pepper and mix well.

Place a wonton wrapper on a work surface (keep remaining wrappers covered). Dip a fingertip in water and moisten two sides of the wrapper. Place 1 teaspoon of the pork mixture in the center of the wrapper, and then fold the wrapper over to form a triangle, enclosing the filling. Press firmly to seal the edges. Moisten one lower tip of the triangle, bring the opposite tip around, and press the tips together, sealing securely. Lightly fold back the remaining tip. Set aside. Repeat until all the filling is used.

Preheat the oven to 200°F. Set a cooling rack on a rimmed baking sheet and place near the stove. Pour canola oil to a depth of 4 inches into a heavy, deep pot. Warm the oil over medium-high heat until it reaches 350°F on a deep-frying thermometer. A few at a time, fry the wontons in the hot oil, turning them once or twice with a wire skimmer, until lightly browned, 1–2 minutes. Transfer the wontons to the rack and place in the oven. Always allow the oil to return to 350°F before adding more.

In a small serving bowl, stir together the chile sauce and remaining 4 tablespoons soy sauce. Place on a platter alongside the wontons, and serve right away.

MAKES 45–50 WONTONS

New World match

A bubbly from Tasmania, Australia's coolest wine region, makes a finely textured foil for the salty and spicy flavors here.

Old World match

A dry sparkling Vouvray will cut through the fat of the wonton and tamp down the sauce's heat.

Alternative pairings

Try a lightly fizzy Vinho Verde (Crisp Whites, page 53) for a refreshing match.

The slight sweetness of a German Kabinett Riesling from Mosel (Soft Whites, page 68) will offset the dish's salty and spicy flavors.

Parmesan-hazelnut coins

A fruity, bubbly sparkling wine counteracts the richness in these cheesy, buttery hors d'oeuvres. A wine with a toasty character will harmonize well with the hazelnuts.

In a food processor, combine the cheese and ½ cup of the hazelnuts and pulse several times until the cheese and nuts are in fine, uniform pieces but not pulverized. Add the flour, baking powder, paprika, salt, mustard, and pepper, and pulse once or twice to combine with the cheese and nuts. Add the butter pieces and pulse until they are the size of small peas. With the motor running, gradually add 2 tablespoons of the ice water. Then add as much of the remaining 1 tablespoon water, 1 teaspoon at a time, as needed for the dough to come together in a ball.

Remove the dough from the processor, divide it in half, and place each half on a large piece of plastic wrap. Roll each half into a log 1½ inches in diameter. Wrap each log in the plastic wrap and refrigerate for at least 1 hour or up to 2 days.

Preheat the oven to 350°F. Line 2 large rimmed baking sheets with parchment paper.

Chop the remaining ½ cup hazelnuts into small pieces. Slice each dough log into rounds about ⅛ inch thick. Place the rounds on the prepared baking sheets, spacing them 1 inch apart. Lightly paint a ½-inch-wide stripe of egg white down the center of each round. Sprinkle some chopped hazelnuts on each stripe, and gently press into place with a fingertip.

Bake the coins until firm and golden around the edges, 8–10 minutes. Transfer the rounds to wire racks and cool slightly. Arrange on a platter and serve warm.

MAKES ABOUT 60 COINS

¼ lb Parmesan cheese, cut into 1-inch cubes

1 cup hazelnuts, toasted and skinned

1¼ cups all-purpose flour

½ tsp baking powder

½ tsp sweet paprika

½ tsp kosher salt

¼ tsp dry mustard

⅛ tsp ground white pepper or cayenne pepper

½ cup cold unsalted butter, cut into 6 equal pieces

2–3 tbsp ice water

1 egg white, lightly beaten

New World match

The toastiness of a lees-aged California Blanc de Blancs will flatter both the nuts and the cheese.

Old World match

A rich nonvintage Brut Champagne will mirror the hazelnut's toasty flavors, even as it cleanses the palate.

Alternative pairings

An off-dry Loire rosé (Pink Wines, page 99) will provide a lightly sweet counterpoint to the coins' saltiness.

A tangy Barbera from Piedmont (Juicy Reds, page 113) will emphasize the cheese's savoriness.

Brandade on crostini

The wine's crisp effervescence counteracts both the creaminess and saltiness of the spread. The sensation of crunch imparted by the toasts is similar to that of the wine's bubbles in the mouth.

1 lb salt cod fillet, preferably in thick pieces

1 cup whole milk

1 small yellow onion, thinly sliced

6 black peppercorns

1 bay leaf

1 fresh thyme sprig

1 slice fresh ginger

2 or 3 fresh flat-leaf parsley sprigs

6 oz Yukon gold potato, peeled and thinly sliced

Kosher salt and freshly ground black pepper

About 3/4 cup half-and-half

3 cloves garlic, minced

2 tsp minced shallot

2 tbsp heavy cream

2 tbsp extra-virgin olive oil

Pinch *each* of ground white pepper and freshly grated nutmeg

About 40 baguette slices, 1/4 inch thick, toasted

To prepare the cod, place it in a bowl with water to cover and refrigerate for 24 hours, changing the water several times. Taste the water, and if it tastes only lightly salty, drain the cod. If the water still tastes very salty, soak the cod for another 12 hours, again changing the water a few times, and then drain. Preheat the oven to 350°F.

In a saucepan over medium heat, combine the cod, 3 cups water, the milk, onion, peppercorns, bay leaf, thyme, ginger, and parsley. Bring just to a boil, then reduce the heat to low, cover, and simmer until the fish just starts to flake when pierced with a knife tip, about 10 minutes. Remove from the heat and let the fish stand in the liquid for 10 minutes.

While the salt cod is cooking, arrange the potato slices in an even layer in the bottom of a wide, ovenproof saucepan. Season with salt and black pepper and pour in enough half-and-half almost to cover the potatoes. Place over medium heat, bring to a boil, cover, and place in the oven. Bake until the potatoes are tender when pierced with a knife tip, about 20 minutes. Remove from the oven.

Drain the salt cod and break it into rough 1-inch chunks, removing any errant bones or bits of skin. In a food processor, combine the salt cod, garlic, and shallot and process until the mixture is crumbly. Add the potatoes, cream, oil, 1/2 teaspoon salt, and the white pepper and nutmeg and process until the mixture is well combined but still has a little texture. Taste and adjust the seasoning.

Arrange the toasted baguette slices on a platter with the brandade for spreading. Serve right away.

MAKES ABOUT 2¼ CUPS, OR ENOUGH FOR ABOUT 40 TOASTS

New World match

Consider a lighthearted Kiwi sparkler—New Zealand's best-kept wine secret—as a great partner for all manner of salty hors d'oeuvres.

Old World match

For a Mediterranean-inspired match, serve the silky brandade with a Spanish Cava.

Alternative pairings

A fruity, acidic Albariño from Galicia (Crisp Whites, page 53) will nicely contrast with the salty spread.

Red wine fans will love the way a simple Beaujolais (Juicy Reds, page 112) plays off the salty fish.

Smoked chicken salad

The crisp texture and acidic tang of this salad are echoed by those of the wine. Toasty walnut oil and smoked chicken help form a link to a wine that features toasty or nutty aromas.

2 tsp Dijon mustard

2 tsp Champagne vinegar

3 tbsp extra-virgin olive oil

1 tbsp walnut oil

3 tbsp chopped fresh tarragon

¼ tsp sugar

¼ tsp kosher salt

Freshly ground black pepper

4 heads Belgian endive, 2 red and 2 white, about 2½ oz each

¼ lb boneless smoked chicken

In a small bowl, whisk together the mustard, vinegar, olive oil, walnut oil, 1 tablespoon tarragon, the sugar, salt, and pepper to taste to make a dressing. Cover and refrigerate until ready to serve, up to 4 hours.

Trim off the base of each endive and separate the leaves. Cut the leaves crosswise into 1–2 inch pieces and place in a bowl. Cut the chicken into bite-sized pieces about the same size as the endive pieces. Add the chicken to the endive.

Just before serving, toss the salad with enough of the dressing to coat the chicken and endive lightly; you may not need all of it. Divide the salad among chilled individual plates. Garnish each salad with the remaining 2 tablespoons tarragon and serve right away.

MAKES 4 SERVINGS

New World match

Opt for a cool-climate sparkling wine from the Pacific Northwest of the U.S., whose extra acidity will take the edge off the tart vinegar.

Old World match

A fruity Crémant from Alsace will nicely echo the dressing's hint of sweetness.

Alternative pairings

A Sauvignon Blanc from New Zealand (Crisp Whites, page 52) can handle the dressing's mustardy tang.

This light dish will match a light Alsatian-style Riesling from Australia's Clare Valley (Soft Whites, page 68).

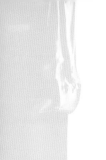

Smoked salmon scramble on country bread

The wine's bubbles and acid counter the richness of the smoked salmon and cream cheese in this brunch dish. Serving the eggs on toast lends more texture and links them to toasty wines.

Preheat the oven to 325°F.

Mix together the olive oil and melted butter and brush on both sides of the bread slices. Place the slices on a baking sheet and bake, turning once, until golden brown on both sides, about 15 minutes.

Meanwhile, in a 10-inch nonstick frying pan over medium-low heat, melt the butter. Add the onion and sauté until translucent and soft, about 5 minutes. While the onion is cooking, in a bowl, whisk together the eggs, the half-and-half, 1 tablespoon dill, and a little salt and pepper. Add the salmon to the frying pan and stir to combine with the onion. Add the egg mixture and stir until the eggs begin to set, 3–4 minutes. Distribute the cream cheese evenly over the eggs and continue to cook and stir until the eggs are barely set but still creamy, 1–2 minutes longer.

Place a piece of bread on each of four warmed plates and top with the egg mixture, dividing evenly. Garnish each plate with a small amount of minced dill and serve right away.

MAKES 4 SERVINGS

1 tbsp extra-virgin olive oil

1 tbsp unsalted butter, melted

4 slices coarse country bread, about ¾ inch thick

2 tbsp unsalted butter

1 small yellow onion, chopped

4 eggs

2 tbsp half-and-half

1 tbsp minced fresh dill, plus more for garnish

Kosher salt and freshly ground black pepper

3 oz smoked salmon, diced

2 tbsp finely diced cream cheese

New World matches

A North Coast sparkling rosé from California will match both the pink hue and creamy flavor of this rich egg dish.

For a more up-front, fruity pink bubbly, consider a Blanc de Noirs from Napa or Sonoma.

Old World match

The elegantly muted fruit of a vintage rosé Champagne is the perfect choice for a special-occasion brunch.

Alternative pairing

A Riesling from the Finger Lakes (Soft Whites, page 68) will serve as a tasty foil for the salmon-spiked eggs.

Shrimp & chorizo skewers with couscous

The sweet, rich shrimp and smoky chorizo lay the foundation for a pleasing contrast with the acidic wine. The texture of the spiced couscous mimics that of the wine's bubbles.

1 lb large shrimp, peeled and deveined

2 tbsp extra-virgin olive oil

2 tbsp fresh lemon juice

2 cloves minced garlic

1/2 tsp ground cumin

Kosher salt and freshly ground black pepper

8 small piquillo peppers (from a jar or can), or 2 medium-sized roasted red bell peppers, peeled

3/4 lb fully cooked Spanish chorizo sausage, about 1 inch in diameter, cut into slices 1/3 inch thick

1/3 cup pine nuts

1 1/2 cups reduced-sodium chicken broth

3 tbsp extra-virgin olive oil

1/2 tsp ground cumin

1 1/2 cups instant couscous

1/3 cup golden raisins

2 tbsp chopped fresh cilantro

Soak 25–30 wooden sandwich picks or small bamboo skewers in water to cover for 30 minutes. In a large bowl, combine the shrimp, oil, lemon juice, garlic, and cumin and a pinch each of salt and black pepper and mix well. Cover and refrigerate for 30 minutes.

Cut the peppers lengthwise into strips 3/4–1 inch wide and 2 1/2 inches long. Wrap 1 piece of pepper around the middle of each slice of chorizo and set aside. Remove the shrimp from the marinade, and discard the marinade. Stand a slice of pepper-wrapped chorizo on its edge and place it in the center of a shrimp. Thread a skewer through the shrimp and chorizo, catching both the head and tail of the shrimp. Repeat with the remaining shrimp and chorizo. Refrigerate until ready to grill.

Prepare a charcoal or gas grill for direct-heat cooking over high heat.

In a small, dry frying pan over medium heat, toast the pine nuts, shaking the pan often, until golden and fragrant, about 2 minutes. Transfer to a small plate. In a small saucepan over high heat, bring the broth, olive oil, 1 teaspoon salt, and the cumin to a boil over high heat. Pour in the couscous, cover, remove from the heat, and let stand for 5 minutes. Fluff the couscous with a fork, and then gently stir in the raisins and toasted pine nuts; keep warm.

Just before you're ready to serve, grill the skewers, turning once halfway through grilling, until the shrimp turn pink and are just firm to the touch, 3–4 minutes total. Be careful not to overcook. Arrange the couscous on a warmed serving platter. Arrange the skewers on top, garnish with the cilantro, and serve right away.

MAKES 25–30 SKEWERS

New World match

A Cap Classique Brut, South Africa's answer to Champagne, will help link the shellfish with the sausage.

Old World matches

Try a dry German Sekt, whose high acidity will help cut the fat of the chorizo and at the same time flatter the shrimp.

If you prefer a light and refreshing contrast to the dish's sweet-savory flavors, reach for a fruity but dry Prosecco.

Alternative pairing

Pour a juicy, young Albariño (Crisp Whites, page 53) for a Spanish-inspired contrast.

Crisp whites

Fresh, pleasingly acidic, and thirst quenching, crisp whites boast a light body and a refreshing finish. With little or no oak aging, these wines pair well with a wide variety of foods.

Crisp white wines hail from all over the world, but perhaps the best known to the U.S. market are made from Sauvignon Blanc or Pinot Grigio grapes. Crisp whites are thought to be among the most food friendly of all wine styles, complementing or contrasting a long list of ingredients. For this reason, a crisp-style white is a good bet if you are ordering for a group of white-wine drinkers in a restaurant. These wines are perfect for serving at a cocktail party, to drink alone as a thirst quencher or to match with an array of different types of hors d'oeuvres. Crisp whites are best served well chilled to bring out their thirst-slaking attributes.

About crisp whites

Crisp whites are characterized by fresh, springlike aromas, a light mouthfeel, and pronounced acidity. Considered perfect quaffing wines precisely because they are so refreshing, crisp whites also pair extremely well with food. These wines can take on sour, bitter, or spicy foods with ease, as well as "problem" ingredients, such as salads and asparagus, that other wines have trouble standing up to.

Stainless steel fermentation

Most winemakers who make crisp whites ferment the wines in stainless-steel tanks instead of oak barrels. This gives the wine-maker better control over the fermentation temperature and ensures that the flavors remain crisp and bright (aging in oak would add toasty flavor, a rounder texture, and tannins to the wine). Often, stainless-steel fermentation takes place under cold temperatures, which better preserves a wine's distinct fruity and herbaceous flavors.

Attributes of crisp whites

Crisp whites feature pronounced acidity, often coupled with "green," vegetal aromas and occasionally a hint of fizz. Good acidity is prized in all crisp whites, but it shouldn't overwhelm the mouth. Not enough acidity and a wine can taste dull, but a wine that is too acidic is considered out of balance. You want to think "zesty" and "zingy," not "sharp" and "sour" when you sample a crisp white wine. Experts claim that the distinct acidity of crisp whites actually helps food taste better—think of how a squeeze of lemon on a simply cooked fish fillet brings out the fish's flavor. Because of their clean flavors, crisp white wines can also help counter foods that are very rich, helping to cleanse your mouth after eating dishes with fatty ingredients.

In general, crisp whites work well with light foods, as their light body forms a match based on complementary textures. You can also pair crisp whites with rich foods to make an intriguing contrast, but take care that the rich food isn't so powerful that it overwhelms the wine, and add companion ingredients to form a stronger link between the two partners. Crisp whites match well to salty or briny foods, forming a bracing contrast with such things as oysters or green olives. Crisp whites can also be paired successfully with acidic foods or salad dressings, as the acidity of the wine helps cancel out the sharpness of vinegar.

1 Look

Crisp white wines are usually very pale in color, sometimes even with a tinge of green. In general, a light color indicates a young wine and cold fermentation (though there are exceptions) which are preferred qualities in crisp white wines.

2 Swirl

Crisp whites are typically low to moderate in alcohol, which corresponds to the wine's body. As you swirl the wine in the glass you will probably see that the legs are on the thin side and disappear relatively quickly. The wine will appear thin.

3 Smell

The alluring aromas in crisp wines evoke tart fruit or green vegetables, hinting at the wine's high acidity. Fresh herbs, grass or hay, and a suggestion of minerals are also common in wines of this style.

4 Sip

The flavors of crisp whites are similar to the aromas—bright and straightforward. The wine will feel light in the mouth, closer to skim milk than cream. The amount of time the flavor lingers on the tongue can vary depending on the grape or winemaker, but it will probably be on the short side. The overall impression of the wine will be refreshing.

Flavor profile

Crisp whites from the Old World lean toward the austere. Expect clean finishes and mineral notes, even some hints of chalk and yeast. Crisp whites from the New World tend to be racier, with more pronounced vegetal flavors and layers of citrus and tropical fruits. Regardless of their individual attributes, crisp whites will be light in texture, young in age, and invigorating.

Mint

A number of crisp whites boast a clean, minty aroma and flavor, which enhance a wine's refreshing qualities.

Green apple

A green-apple flavor comes from the natural malic acid present in grapes. It is the same acid that makes apples taste so tart.

Lime

The snappy acidity in some Spanish, Portuguese, and Italian crisp whites can be described as similar to a squeeze of lime.

Grapefruit

The refreshing, slightly vegetal quality of many Sauvignon Blancs reminds many tasters of a just-cut grapefruit.

Cucumber

The clean, slightly "green" flavor found in many crisp whites is often compared to a crisp cucumber.

Minerals

The mineral-rich soil of many Old World vineyards contributes a chalky impression in many cool-climate whites.

Asparagus

Some tasters claim they can detect the aroma of the green vegetable in a New World Sauvignon Blanc. Perhaps for this reason, the wine is one of the few that can be paired successfully with asparagus.

Herbs

Many crisp whites smell and taste of fresh herbs, which complements the green, vegetal flavors of the wine.

Lemon

Often found in cool-climate white wines, a lemony aroma and flavor comes from a wine's citric acid.

Grass

If green were a flavor, it could be used to describe wines made from the Sauvignon Blanc grape, particularly those made in New Zealand and California, which are often described as "grassy."

Key crisp white wines

The best crisp whites historically came from cool climates, where the grapes could remain on the vine for long periods of time to develop their natural acidity. Today, modern winemaking methods allow greater temperature and quality control, so even grapes grown in hot climates are being made into refreshingly crisp, dry white wines. Look for young vintages with an alcohol content less than 12.5 percent.

Estate bottled

Seen on many wine labels, the term "estate bottled" is legally defined in the United States as wine made from grapes owned by the winery, or from a vineyard that is totally under the winery's control and is located in the same appellation. In France, this phrase appears as *mis en bouteille au chateau,* and indicates that the wine is made from grapes that are grown on the winery estate. These two terms, particularly in the Old World, can indicate a superior wine, although many fine wines exist that are not bottled on the winery estate.

Sauvignon Blanc

Sauvignon Blanc is an extremely versatile grape and can be vinified in a number of ways. In France, the crisp style of Sauvignon Blanc is best represented by the Loire Valley, where it forms Pouilly Fumé and Sancerre, both known for "green" and flinty aromas. In the New World, California has a reputation for outstanding Sauvignon Blanc–based wines, which are punctuated by more grassy, less minerally aromas than their French cousins. Standouts include wines from Napa, Sonoma, and Mendocino, among other regions. Washington State also produces elegant examples of New World Sauvignon Blanc. Even more pungent are wines from New Zealand, which has forged its own distinctive, racy style redolent of wild herbs and tropical fruit. Other countries producing quality Sauvignon Blanc–based wines in a crisp style include Chile, Australia, South Africa, and cool regions of Italy. Look for a fuller style of Sauvignon Blanc in the Rich Whites chapter (page 83).

Pinot Grigio

In Italy, vintners harvest crisp, appley Pinot Grigio grapes when they are just shy of full maturity to make their light, easy-drinking white wine. This light, fresh wine has also recently caught on in California, where it is fast gaining on Chardonnay in popularity. You can also find Pinot Grigio made in a softer, more aromatic style, usually referred to by its French name, Pinot Gris, in the Soft Whites chapter (page 69).

Muscadet

Also called "Melon de Bourgogne," this light, zesty wine is the classic companion to oysters harvested along the Atlantic coastline adjacent to the Loire Valley. Some of the best examples of Muscadet are labeled *"sur lie,"* meaning they have been left in contact with the lees (mainly dead yeast cells), which lends more complexity in flavor.

Chablis

Made from the Chardonnay grape in northern Burgundy, Chablis features the flinty, stony flavors of the regional soil layered with crisp fruit flavors. Chablis is not aged in oak, so the wine retains its pure taste. Avoid the mass-marketed "California Chablis," which is low quality and has little character. Like Muscadet, Chablis is a classic companion to oysters and other shellfish. The same grape is often vinified in a fuller, toastier style; look for it in the Rich Whites chapter (page 82).

Albariño

Albariño is grown primarily in northwest Spain, notably in the Rias Baixas region of Galicia, where it makes wines of varying styles. A young Albariño will supply the desired acidity when you want a crisp white wine; older bottles become richer and creamier with age, losing their bright acidity. Next door, in Portugal, the grape is called Alvarinho. There it is made into a light, acidic, low-alcohol wine with a slight effervescence called Vinho Verde. Although some claim the color has a hint of green, the name "verde," meaning green in Portuguese, does not so much refer to the color of the wine but to the fact that the wine is released in the spring, which is considered the greening of the year.

White Rioja

Rioja, a wine-growing region in Spain, makes clean-tasting whites made from Macabeo, or Viura, grapes. Look for a youthful bottle if you desire a crisp style. Riojas are also available aged in oak, but their rounder, fuller qualities bend them into Rich Whites (page 83).

Pinot Bianco

Lean and snappy, the best types of Pinot Bianco come from northern Italy. The grape can also be referred to by its French name, Pinot Blanc, but it is usually vinified in a different style, more appropriate to the Soft Whites chapter (page 69).

Soave

This simple Italian table wine, popular in the Veneto region, is made primarily from Garganega grapes. Some winemakers also include Chardonnay, Pinot Bianco, and other grapes to lend more body.

Pairing wine with salad

Salad is often considered a problem food when pairing it with wine. The culprit is usually the vinegar used in the salad dressing, which, if too sharp, can make wines taste unpleasant. If you want to pair salad with wine, keep in mind the following guidelines: Choose a mild vinegar, preferably one made from wine, or use lemon or lime juice in the dressing. Next, add nuts, cheese, vegetables, or meat to reinforce the wine match. Finally, pair the salad with a light, high-acid white wine that is not too complex.

Fava bean crostini

Because of their green, vegetal character, fava beans pair well with a crisp white with similar flavors. The wine's acidity tempers the salty, tangy, pecorino-cheese topping.

CROSTINI

2 tbsp unsalted butter, melted

2 tbsp extra-virgin olive oil

About 35 slices sweet baguette, 1/4 inch thick

1 1/4 lb fava beans, shelled, or 1 cup thawed, frozen shelled edamame

1/3 cup extra-virgin olive oil

1 large clove garlic, minced

1 tbsp fresh lemon juice

1/2 tsp kosher salt

3 or 4 dashes hot red or green pepper sauce such as Tabasco

Freshly ground black pepper

4 tbsp chopped fresh mint

2-oz wedge pecorino romano or Parmesan cheese

To make the crostini, preheat the oven to 300°F. In a small bowl, stir together the butter and the 2 tablespoons oil. Brush both sides of each baguette slice with the mixture and place the slices on a rimmed baking sheet. Place in the oven and toast, turning once, until crisp and lightly browned, 10–12 minutes. Remove from the oven and let cool on the pan.

Fill a small saucepan three-fourths full of water and bring to a boil over high heat. Add the fava beans and parboil for 2 minutes. Drain the beans and let cool until they can be handled, about 5 minutes. Pinch each bean to force it from its thin outer skin, discarding the skins. You should have about 1 cup beans. (If you are using edamame, they are ready to use once they have been thawed.)

In a frying pan over low heat, warm the 1/3 cup oil. Add the garlic and cook until fragrant, about 1 minute. Do not allow it to brown. Add the fava beans and sauté until the beans begin to soften, about 5 minutes. Remove from the heat and carefully pour the contents of the pan into a food processor. Add the lemon juice, salt, pepper sauce, and a few grinds of black pepper and process until smooth. If the mixture seems a little stiff, add 1–2 teaspoons of water. Transfer the mixture to a small bowl, taste, and adjust the seasoning, and then stir in 3 tablespoons of the mint.

Spread the warm bean mixture on the crostini and arrange on a platter. Using a vegetable peeler or cheese plane, shave the cheese over the top. Sprinkle with the remaining 1 tablespoon mint and serve right away.

MAKES 30–35 CROSTINI

New World match
A cool-climate New Zealand Sauvignon Blanc offers an abundance of complementary flavors in this garden-fresh pairing.

Old World matches
A mouthwatering Portuguese Vinho Verde makes an appealing partner, and its slightly green color complements that of the fava beans.

Go all-Italian with a fragrant, herbal Pinot Grigio from the Alto Adige, which will nicely reflect the crostini's vegetal flavors.

Alternative pairing
If you're looking for a slightly more subtle match, consider a crisp Tasmanian Champagne-style wine (Sparkling Wines, page 38).

Vegetable lasagna rolls

The bright spring vegetables, tart goat cheese, and sprightly tomato sauce used in this dish call for a crisp white, whose acidity will also help counter the richness of the white sauce.

3 tbsp unsalted butter

½ cup minced onion

3 tbsp all-purpose flour

3 cups whole milk, hot

Kosher salt and freshly ground black pepper

1 tsp Worcestershire sauce

½ tsp dry mustard

½ cup grated Parmesan cheese

Pinch *each* of cayenne pepper and freshly grated nutmeg

2 tbsp extra-virgin olive oil

½ lb cremini mushrooms, thinly sliced

1 tbsp sherry vinegar

1 leek, thinly sliced

⅓ cup slivered fresh basil

1 cup shelled English peas

12 dried lasagna noodles, cooked and cooled

3 oz fresh goat cheese

1 cup prepared tomato sauce

In a saucepan over medium heat, melt the butter. Add the onion and sauté until soft, 3–4 minutes. Whisk in the flour and cook, stirring, until the mixture turns a light golden brown, 4–5 minutes. Gradually add the hot milk, whisking constantly, to make a white sauce. Add 1½ teaspoons salt, the Worcestershire, mustard, cheese, cayenne, and nutmeg and cook, stirring, until thickened, 3–4 minutes. Remove from the heat and set aside.

In a frying pan over medium-high heat, warm 1 tablespoon of the oil. Add the mushrooms, season with salt and pepper, and sauté until light brown, 3–4 minutes. Add the vinegar and cook for 1 minute longer. Transfer the mushrooms to a plate and set aside. Return the pan to medium heat and add the remaining 1 tablespoon oil. Add the leek and sauté until softened, 2–3 minutes. Add the basil and 2 tablespoons water and season lightly with salt and pepper. Cover, reduce the heat to low, and cook until most of the liquid has evaporated, 8–10 minutes. Uncover, remove from the heat, and stir in the peas, mushrooms, and 1 cup of the white sauce.

Preheat the oven to 350°F. Oil a 9-inch square baking dish. Spread about 1 cup of the white sauce in the bottom of the prepared dish. Spoon about 3 tablespoons of the vegetable mixture along the length of a lasagna noodle, leaving about 1 inch uncovered at one end. Crumble a little of the goat cheese over the filling. Roll up the noodle into a compact bundle, then stand the roll vertically in the dish. Repeat with the remaining noodles, filling, and cheese. Spoon the remaining white sauce over the tops of the lasagna rolls. Distribute the tomato sauce evenly over the white sauce. Lightly tent the dish with aluminum foil.

Bake the lasagna for 30 minutes. Uncover and continue baking until the sauce is hot and bubbling, 10–15 minutes longer. Let the lasagna rest for 10 minutes before serving.

MAKES 4–6 SERVINGS

New World match

The ripe flavors of a Pinot Grigio from California's Central Coast will flatter the lasagna's tomato sauce and peas, even as they play off the goat cheese inside.

Old World match

A northeastern Italian Pinot Bianco has the requisite acidity to smooth out the tang of both the sauce and the cheese without overpowering the dish's subtle flavors.

Alternative pairings

A Sangiovese Rosé from California's North Coast (Pink Wines, page 99) offers tastes that both complement and contrast with this dish.

A medium-bodied Barbera from north-western Italy (Smooth Reds, page 127) has a natural affinity for all sorts of creamy, tomato-based dishes.

Sautéed sole with fennel & lemon compote

Fennel and lemon are typical flavors in crisp whites, forming an easy complement for this dish. The richness from the panko breading helps form a pleasing contrast to the acidic wine.

To make the compote, trim off the stalks and feathery fronds from the fennel bulbs, discarding the stalks and reserving the fronds. Cut the bulbs in half lengthwise, then cut crosswise into slices ¼ inch thick.

In a saucepan over medium heat, melt the butter. Add the fennel slices and the ½ teaspoon salt and sauté until the fennel is lightly browned, 3–4 minutes. Add the wine, lemon zest and juice, and sugar and toss with the fennel until evenly distributed. Cover the pan, reduce the heat to low, and cook until the fennel is very soft, 5–6 minutes. Remove the pan from the heat and keep warm.

Divide the oil between 2 large frying pans and heat over medium-high heat. Meanwhile, spread the *panko* on a large, shallow plate. On another shallow plate, whisk together the egg, pepper sauce, the ¼ teaspoon salt, and a few grinds of pepper until blended. Spread the flour on a third large plate. When the oil is hot, lightly flour a fish fillet on both sides, dip it into the egg mixture, and then dip it into the *panko*, coating both sides evenly. Gently place the breaded fillet into the hot oil and, working quickly, repeat with the remaining fillets. Sauté the fillets until nicely browned and crisp on the first side, about 3 minutes. Turn the fillets over and sauté until the second side is browned and crisp and the fish is opaque throughout when tested with a knife tip, about 2 minutes longer.

Transfer the fillets to warmed individual plates and spoon a mound of the compote alongside. Sprinkle with the parsley and serve right away.

MAKES 4 SERVINGS

New World match

Try a lemony, cool-climate Sauvignon Blanc from Chile's Casablanca Valley to complement similar citrus flavors in the compote.

Old World matches

A tangy Albariño from Galicia in northwestern Spain is a refreshing choice from Europe.

Unoaked Chablis or Muscadet are fine foils for just about any type of seafood that is flavored with citrus.

Alternative pairing

A modest Grüner Veltliner (Soft Whites, page 69), with its peppery, vegetal flavors matches beautifully with simply prepared fin fish.

COMPOTE

2 fennel bulbs, about 1 lb each

3 tbsp unsalted butter

½ tsp kosher salt

¼ cup crisp white wine

Zest of 1 lemon, finely grated

1 tbsp fresh lemon juice

2 tsp sugar

⅓ cup canola oil

1¾ cups panko (Japanese bread crumbs)

1 egg

2 or 3 drops hot red pepper sauce such as Tabasco

¼ tsp kosher salt

Freshly ground black pepper

2 tbsp all-purpose flour

4 fillets of sole, about 6 oz each

2 tbsp chopped fresh flat-leaf parsley

Chicken breasts stuffed with olives & fontina

The piquant flavor of green olives pairs effortlessly with crisp whites. But the beauty of this match lies in the contrast of the crisp chicken skin and gooey fontina cheese with the lively wine.

4 skin-on, boneless chicken breast halves, about 1/2 lb each

1 cup coarsely shredded fontina cheese

1/4 cup chopped pimiento-stuffed green olives

2 tbsp grated Parmesan cheese

2 tsp extra-virgin olive oil

Kosher salt and freshly ground pepper

1/4 cup crisp white wine

Preheat the oven to 400°F. Using a small, sharp knife and starting at the thickest side, cut a pocket in each chicken breast, extending it to within 1/2 inch of each side and being careful not to cut all the way through the breast. In a small bowl, combine the fontina, olives, and Parmesan and mix well. Stuff each breast with one-fourth of the cheese mixture and secure the opening closed with a wooden pick.

Brush the stuffed breasts on both sides with the olive oil, and then season on both sides with salt and pepper. Place the breasts, skin side up, in a shallow glass baking dish or nonreactive pan just large enough to hold them and pour the wine into the dish.

Bake the chicken breasts until the skin is crisp and an instant-read thermometer inserted into the thickest part of a breast registers 170°F, 30–35 minutes.

Remove from the oven and let cool slightly. Transfer to warmed individual plates and serve right away.

MAKES 4 SERVINGS

New World match

For a tasty change of pace, consider serving a lively Argentine *Torrontes,* which is similar to an Albariño.

Old World match

For an elegant match that suggests both regional and flavor affinities, try a young Soave Classico.

Alternative pairings

If you'd prefer a red with this dish, try a fruity Loire Valley Cabernet Franc (Juicy Reds, page 113). The wine's earthiness and tang will play nicely off both the olives and the cheese.

For a slightly more robust match, consider serving a northern Italian Dolcetto (Juicy Reds, page 113). Its modest tannins will be softened by the dish's rich cheese filling.

Grilled mahimahi with tomatillo sauce

Here the main ingredient forms a neutral base for the sauce. A crisp white will stand up well to the sauce's tangy tomatillos, herbal cilantro, bright lime juice, and bold jalapeños.

3 or 4 tomatillos, about 5 oz total weight

4 green onions, including about 6 inches of the green tops

1 tbsp plus 1 tsp extra-virgin olive oil, plus oil for brushing

1 small clove garlic, finely chopped

1/2 small avocado, peeled and coarsely chopped

1/3 cup lightly packed chopped fresh cilantro leaves and tender stems

1 tbsp fresh lime juice

1 tsp honey

1 tsp finely chopped jalapeño chile, or to taste

Kosher salt

4 mahimahi fillets, 6–7 oz each

Freshly ground black pepper

Prepare a charcoal or gas grill for direct-heat cooking over high heat, or preheat the broiler.

Discard the papery husks from the tomatillos, rinse them under cold water, and pat dry with paper towels. Brush the tomatillos and green onions with the 1 teaspoon oil and place on the grill rack. Cook the vegetables, turning once or twice, until lightly charred on both sides, 4–5 minutes total for the onions and 6–8 minutes total for the tomatillos. The tomatillos will have softened and started to release their juices.

Transfer the tomatillos to a food processor and the green onions to a cutting board. Coarsely chop the onions and add to the food processor along with the garlic, avocado, cilantro, the remaining 1 tablespoon oil, the lime juice, honey, chile, and 1/2 teaspoon salt. Process until the mixture is smooth. Transfer to a bowl, then taste and adjust the seasoning with lime juice and/or salt.

Lightly brush the fish fillets on both sides with oil and then season on both sides with salt and pepper. Place the fillets on the grill rack. Cook, turning once about halfway through cooking, until opaque throughout when tested with a knife tip, 8–10 minutes total.

Transfer the fillets to warmed individual plates. Spoon the sauce over the fish, dividing evenly, and serve right away.

MAKES 4 SERVINGS

New World matches

With its long growing season and cool climate, Washington State is a reliable source for herbal Sauvignon Blanc, which matches this dish's piquant green flavors.

This zesty sauce calls for an equally sprightly wine, like an unoaked New Zealand Chardonnay, which is akin to Chablis, to stand up to its potent mixture of flavors.

Old World match

Choose an unoaked young white Rioja (or a similar white wine from the nearby Rueda region). The Spanish partner is a perfect foil for the south-of-the-border sauce.

Alternative pairing

A refreshing California Blanc de Blancs (Sparkling Wines, page 39) will help cool the spice in the sauce.

Pork with salsa verde

This vibrant sauce cuts the richness of pork and echoes the brisk acid and herbal aromas of crisp whites. The recipe is based on a dish from Italy, which is renowned for whites in the crisp style.

1/4 cup pine nuts

1 clove garlic, peeled

2 green onions, white parts only

9 tbsp extra-virgin olive oil

1/4 cup capers, rinsed

1 tbsp anchovy paste

2 tsp Dijon mustard

1 tbsp fresh lemon juice

1/2 tsp sugar

Kosher salt

Freshly ground white pepper

1/2 cup tightly packed flat-leaf parsley leaves

1 pork tenderloin, 1–1 1/4 lb, trimmed

1/3 cup all-purpose flour

Freshly ground black pepper

2 eggs

3 cups fresh bread crumbs

4 tbsp unsalted butter

To make the *salsa verde*, in a small, dry frying pan over medium heat, toast the nuts, shaking the pan often, until golden and fragrant, 3–4 minutes. Transfer to a small plate. With the motor running in a food processor, drop the garlic and green onions through the feed tube and process until finely chopped. Scrape down the sides of the bowl. Add 5 tablespoons of the oil, the capers, anchovy paste, mustard, lemon juice, sugar, and a pinch each of salt and white pepper and process until smooth. Add the parsley and nuts and pulse 8–10 times to combine. Transfer to a bowl, taste, and adjust the seasonings; set aside.

Cut the pork tenderloin crosswise into 8 cutlets, each 1 1/2–1 3/4 inches thick. Place each cutlet between 2 sheets of plastic wrap. Using the flat side of a meat pounder, gently flatten each piece until it is an even 1/4 inch thick. In a large, shallow bowl, stir together the flour, 1/2 teaspoon salt, and a few grinds of black pepper. In a second bowl, beat the eggs until blended. Spread the bread crumbs on a plate. Lightly coat a pork cutlet with the flour mixture on both sides, dip it into the egg mixture, and then dip it into the bread crumbs, coating both sides evenly. Set aside on a large platter. Repeat to coat the remaining pork cutlets.

Place 2 large frying pans over medium-high heat and add 2 tablespoons each of the remaining oil and the butter to each pan. When the butter stops foaming, carefully place the pork cutlets in the pans and sauté until golden brown on the first side, 3–4 minutes. Turn the cutlets over and sauté until the second side is golden brown, 3–4 minutes longer.

Transfer the cutlets to warmed individual plates, placing 2 on each plate. Serve right away with a little of the sauce spooned over each portion.

MAKES 4 SERVINGS

New World match

To handle the mixture of pungent flavors in the sauce, seek out an ultracrisp white, such as a South African Sauvignon Blanc from the Stellenbosch region.

Old World matches

With its green apple and herb flavors, a Pinot Grigio from Friuli, Italy, is a fine choice for this vibrant dish.

A crisp Sauvignon Blanc from Italy's Alto Adige region will also make a fitting partner.

Alternative pairing

In deference to this dish's Italian heritage, consider a dry Prosecco (Sparkling Wines, page 39). Its refreshing effervescence forms a flavorful foil for both the rich breaded pork and the piquant sauce.

Soft whites

Floral, honeyed, and accented by pleasing acidity, soft whites range from dry to slightly sweet. They are perfect partners to a range of foods, including hard-to-match Asian dishes.

The best examples of soft white wines come from cool climates, where the grapes can gain a good amount of acidity on the vine. Riesling and Gewürztraminer wines are the most revered in this category, and growers all over the globe are emulating the classic styles from Germany and northern France. Soft whites are available in a range of dryness levels, but the best affinity with food usually occurs with a dry or slightly off-dry wine. Perfect as aperitifs, soft whites are also a good match for the layered flavors of Thai, Vietnamese, or Chinese cuisines. Avoid wines labeled "late harvest," unless you want to pair them with dessert (for sweet wines, turn to page 153).

About soft whites

Like many other white wines, soft whites feature floral aromas, engaging fruitiness, and a backbone of acidity. But what distinguishes soft whites from other styles is their inherent balance and velvety texture. In addition, a hard-to-define quality makes many soft whites taste not quite dry, but not quite sweet, either. Soft whites have little or no oak aging, so the true flavors of the grapes really shine through in the wines.

Residual sugar & dryness

Residual sugar refers to the total amount of sugar remaining in a wine after fermentation, expressed as a percentage of grams per liter. The term "dry" describes wines in which there is no discernible sweetness, or less than 0.5 percent residual sugar (most people begin to perceive sweetness when the residual sugar reaches 0.5 percent). The term "off dry" refers to wines that are slightly sweet, or have between 0.5 and 3.0 percent residual sugar. A wine containing more than 3 percent residual sugar is considered "sweet."

Attributes of soft whites

Like crisp whites, soft whites are good sipping wines, loved for their velvety, easy-drinking qualities. They are also regarded as great food partners for similar reasons. Soft whites' bracing acidity cuts through rich sauces based on cream or coconut milk, while their slight sweetness—desirable in this style of wine—helps counteract spicy or salty ingredients. The grapes in this category can also make stellar sweet wines (see pages 153–157), but for savory food matches, it's best to stick with wines on the dry end of the sweetness scale.

Germany and northern France have built long-standing traditions on their soft whites, in part because they form striking contrasts with the smoky, salty ingredients typical of the region. For example, Riesling is a traditional partner for *choucroute garni* (sauerkraut with cured meats), a traditional dish of Alsace. For a more offbeat match, try soft whites with sushi or sashimi; the wine's supple mouthfeel complements the texture of the raw fish, while its delicate sweetness counters salty soy sauce and spicy wasabi. Soft whites are also terrific paired with mild fruit salsas or sauces based on peaches, apricots, or pears. Other Asian foods, too, are a wonderful match; thanks to their affinity for the complex flavors of the cuisines, soft whites are commonly featured on wine lists at contemporary Vietnamese, Thai, and Chinese restaurants.

1 Look

With some exceptions, soft whites tend to be pale in color, from almost colorless to light straw. Their absence of color is due, in part, to the fact that soft whites are generally from cool-climate areas (in cool regions colors develop very slowly) and the fact that they are consumed when young (wines tend to darken as they age).

2 Swirl

Soft whites may seem slightly viscous as you move them around the glass, hinting at their medium-bodied structure. As you aerate the wine and the aromas begin to emerge, you may wonder if the wine will be a sweet one.

3 Smell

Soft whites are sometimes called "aromatic whites" because of the perfumed scents that emanate from many of the wines. You may also detect pronounced mineral or kerosene-like scents in some wines.

4 Sip

A sip of a soft white reveals smooth, apricot-honey-floral flavors and a mouth-filling texture. Off-dry wines will taste softly sweet, but even dry wines may seem slightly sugary. The wine's acidity will balance any sweetness and keep it food friendly. The flavor will linger on the tongue for different lengths of time, depending on the wine and alcohol content.

Flavor profile

Soft wines from the Old World tend to have mineral-rich flavors reminiscent of the soil in which they are grown. They can be low in alcohol, sometimes as low as seven percent, which makes them great quaffing wines. Soft whites from the New World often boast more pronounced fruit or floral aromas and may be higher in alcohol, though many winemakers aim to produce wines in the Old-World style.

Melon

Look for a refreshing melon flavor in many crisp whites, especially those made from Chenin Blanc.

Lemon

Typical in cool-climate white wines, a lemony aroma and flavor comes from a wine's citric acid, which lends balance to the wine.

Kiwi fruit

Hints of juicy, green kiwi fruit come through in the aroma and flavor of a variety of soft whites.

Quince

Tasters often compare the aroma of soft white wines to the perfumed scent of quince.

Apricot

If you detect the smell of apricots in a white wine, there's a good chance it is a soft white.

Pear

Soft white wines show tree fruit aromas that are soft and honeyed, closer to pears than the apples common in crisp whites.

Fennel

The grassy, anise-like flavor of fresh fennel is commonly associated with a range of soft whites.

Floral

A range of floral scents are found in soft whites, such as honeysuckle, jasmine, lavender, and roses.

Peach

The aroma and flavor of both Riesling and Gewürztraminer are often compared to fresh peaches.

Key soft white wines

In general, for the best food match, pick soft whites that are dry or off-dry (see page 66), with a low alcohol content and from a recent vintage. This will ensure the wine has a good amount of acidity and soft, pleasing flavors, which will match well to a variety of foods. Germany produces some of the best wines in this category, but the labels can be difficult to decipher; ask a trusted wine merchant for guidance.

Wine acids

The most important naturally occurring acids in wine are tartaric, malic, and citric acids, all of which provide distinct flavors and contribute balance, structure, and aging potential to the wine. In cool-climate wines, such as those you find in the Soft Whites and Crisp Whites chapters, it is not uncommon to find a white crystalline substance floating at the bottom of the bottle or adhering to the cork, caused by deposits of the wine's tartaric acid. These crystals are not harmful, but can be strained out if desired.

Riesling

Riesling excels in cool climates, where the high-acid grape can thrive. This white wine grape is Germany's greatest contribution to the wine world and is grown primarily in vineyards along the Rhine River and its tributaries, including the Mosel River. German wine labels can be confusing, but if you look for a wine labeled *Kabinett,* you can be assured of a quality wine with a dry or off-dry flavor. Alsace, France, also has a reputation for making superior Riesling. Unlike most French wine, Riesling from Alsace will list the varietal name on the label. The wines there are aged in old oak, which does not impart wood flavors, or in stainless steel. In the U.S., Riesling is often labeled "Johannisburg Riesling," which indicates it is made in the dry or off-dry style of German wines. Standout producers are found in California, Washington State, and New York State, particularly in the cool Finger Lakes region. Australia is also an up-and-coming region for the grape. Riesling is also often made into a dessert wine from late-harvest grapes. For more information, turn to the Sweet Wines chapter, page 156.

Gewürztraminer

One of the most distinctive of all the wine grapes, Gewürztraminer is noted for its intensely spicy aromas and flavors (the word "gewürz" means "spice" in German), often compared to the scent of roses accented by cinnamon and cloves. Gewürztraminer tends to be darker in color than other soft whites because the grapes have a pinkish cast, which affects the color of the finished wine. As with Riesling, the best examples of Gewürztraminer come from cool parts of the world. Alsace, France, sets the standard, producing intense, spice-imbued wines. You can also find fine examples of Gewürztaminer in Germany and Austria, which are similar in style to that of Alsace. The New World, too, produces fine Gewürztraminer, particularly in California, Oregon, and New Zealand. Expect New World Gewürztraminer to be less spicy and complex than that of Alsace, closer to a Riesling in flavor. Like Riesling, Gewürztraminer grapes make terrific sweet wines (see page 156).

Chenin Blanc

Chenin Blanc is one of the most versatile grapes in the world, adapting well to many different soils and climates. In the Loire region of France, Chenin Blanc makes impressive off-dry soft whites in the regions of Vouvray and Saumur, redolent of flowers, honey, and a touch of grass. Grown modestly in California, Australia, New Zealand, and South Africa, Chenin Blanc makes wines with an appealing, fruit-forward style. Chenin Blanc can also be found as a sparkling wine (page 39) or sweet wine (page 157).

Grüner Veltliner

The top grape in Austria, Grüner Veltliner was originally produced as a modest table wine and became a mainstay at casual cafés of the rural countryside. Today, Grüner Veltiner has become a darling of the wine world, in part because it is so accessible and food friendly. Many describe Grüner Veltliner's distinctive aroma as fruity with white pepper and green-vegetable nuances ("grüner" means "green" in German) and a minerally backbone, like what you would expect to find in a crisp white (page 49). But Grüner Veltliner is somewhat milder and more multidimensional than Sauvignon Blanc, making it accessible to a wider range of wine drinkers.

Pinot Gris

The standard for Pinot Gris is set in Alsace, France, where it is revered almost as much as Riesling. There it is sometimes called *Tokay–Pinot Gris,* which creates some confusion with sweet wine called Tokay from Hungary. Typically found in an off-dry style, Pinot Gris has an appealing musty flavor. In the New World, Pinot Gris is made in a similar style in Oregon and New Zealand. It is the same grape as Pinot Grigio (see Crisp Whites, page 52), but most wines labeled "Pinot Gris" can be expected to show in the Alsace style.

Pinot Blanc

Although it originated in Burgundy, France, the best examples of Pinot Blanc are now found in Alsace, where it is making increasingly popular wines with apple and spice aromas and appealing weight on the palate. The grape is also widely planted in Germany, where it makes wines in a similar Alsatian style. In the New World, Pinot Blanc is being made with great success in Oregon, whose cool climatic conditions mirror that of Northern Europe. California, too, is producing some interesting wines made from the grape. Pinot Blanc can also be made in a lighter, crisper style, usually called Pinot Bianco, which is popular in Italy (see Crisp Whites, page 53).

Wine & ethnic food

Soft white wines are often recommended by wine experts as apt partners to a range of ethnic foods, such as Chinese, Mexican, Indian, and Southeast Asian dishes. But these pairings did not occur naturally. Beer was the more typical partner, as none of these cuisines emerged in winegrowing areas. That said, the high acid, slight sweetness, and lush texture of this category of wine matches effortlessly to a variety of dishes, including those featuring hot chiles, exotic spices, salty soy sauce, and rich coconut milk.

Bacon & onion tart

This recipe is inspired by a traditional dish from Alsace, France. A combination of smoky bacon and sweet caramelized onions both contrasts and complements a slightly sweet, off-dry wine.

2 slices thick-cut bacon, about 3 oz total weight, cut crosswise into pieces ½ inch wide

1 lb yellow onions, thinly sliced (about 6 cups)

2 tbsp dry white wine

2 tsp fresh thyme leaves

¼ tsp kosher salt

¼ tsp freshly ground black pepper

1 sheet frozen puff pastry, about ½ lb, thawed according to package directions

½ cup coarsely shredded Gruyère or Swiss cheese

3 tbsp freshly grated Parmesan cheese

In a large frying pan over low heat, fry the bacon until it renders its fat and is lightly browned but not crisp, about 4 minutes. Using a slotted spoon, transfer the bacon to paper towels. With the pan still over low heat, add the onions and toss to coat with the bacon fat. Add the wine, thyme, salt, and pepper and stir to combine. Cover and cook, stirring once or twice, until the onions are very soft and lightly browned, about 25 minutes. Uncover, increase the heat to medium, and continue to cook, stirring occasionally, until the liquid has evaporated, 3–4 minutes. The onions should be quite dry. Transfer the onions to a bowl and let stand until slightly cooled, 15–20 minutes.

Meanwhile, preheat the oven to 375°F. Roll out the puff pastry on a sheet of parchment paper into an 11-inch square about ⅛ inch thick. Transfer the parchment and pastry to a rimmed baking sheet. Turn up the pastry edges about ½ inch to make a small raised edge. Prick the pastry all over with the tines of a fork. Bake the pastry until it starts to color but not brown and is dry to the touch, about 10 minutes. Remove from the oven.

Raise the oven temperature to 400°F. Add the Gruyère cheese and the reserved bacon to the cooled onions and mix well. Sprinkle the pastry with the Parmesan cheese, and then spread the onion mixture evenly over the pastry. Bake the tart until the edges of the pastry are lightly browned and a few small brown specks have appeared on the onions, about 20 minutes. Let the tart cool slightly on a cutting board.

Using a sharp knife or a pizza wheel, cut into 3- to 4-inch triangles or squares for a first course, or smaller squares for an appetizer, and divide among individual plates. Serve warm.

MAKES 8 FIRST-COURSE SERVINGS

New World match

A South African Chenin Blanc will highlight the caramelized onions and cut the bacon's fat.

Old World matches

An Alsatian Riesling is a natural partner that will both complement and contrast the tart's tastes and textures.

For another Chenin-based match, try a Vouvray or Saumur Blanc from the Loire.

Alternative pairings

A sparkling Vouvray (Sparkling Wine, page 39) will beautifully counter the bacon's saltiness.

Thai-style green fish curry

A soft white matches the mouthfeel of the coconut milk while the wine's acidity cuts the milk's richness. The chiles in the curry paste are counteracted by the wine's zest and faint sweetness.

1½ lb firm white fish fillets such as halibut, cod, or sea bass, each about 1½ inches thick

1 stalk fresh lemongrass

1 can (13½ fl oz) coconut milk

1 cup reduced-sodium chicken broth

3 tbsp fish sauce

Finely grated zest of 1 lime

3 tbsp fresh lime juice

1 tbsp high-quality green curry paste, preferably Thai Kitchen brand

1 tbsp peeled and grated fresh ginger

1 clove garlic, minced

½ cup chopped fresh cilantro leaves and tender stems

¼ cup chopped fresh basil

2 tbsp chopped fresh mint

2 cups hot cooked jasmine rice or other long-grain white rice

Skin the fish fillets, if necessary, and discard the skin. Cut the fillets into 1½-inch chunks and set aside.

Cut off about 2 inches of the lemongrass stem and pull off and discard the tough outside layers. Finely mince the tender inside stalks, measure out 1 teaspoon, and add it to a saucepan. Add the coconut milk, broth, fish sauce, lime zest and juice, curry paste, ginger, and garlic.

Bring the coconut milk mixture to a boil over medium-high heat, then reduce the heat to low and simmer, uncovered, for about 10 minutes to blend the flavors. Add the fish and simmer gently until the fish is opaque throughout when tested with a knife tip, 4–5 minutes. Add the cilantro, basil, and mint. Taste the curry and adjust the seasonings with fish sauce.

To serve, place a scoop of rice in each of 4 warmed shallow soup bowls and ladle the curry over the rice.

MAKES 4 SERVINGS

New World matches

An off-dry New Zealand Gewürztraminer will echo both the dish's spiciness and sweetness.

An off-dry Gewürz-traminer from the Pacific Northwest also partners deliciously with sweet-spicy dishes.

Old World match

Choose a Mosel Kabinett Riesling for both its touch of sweetness and its racy acidity.

Alternative pairing

A dry Alsace Crémant (Sparkling Wines, page 38) will offset both the fish sauce and the curry.

Steamed mussels with wine & herbs

As the mussels open, their juices mingle with the wine and aromatics to form a naturally complementary sauce. Use the same wine to steam the mussels that you serve with them.

In a large bowl, combine the mussels with water to cover and let stand for 10 minutes. Drain the mussels, then scrub with a brush under running cold water. Remove any beards (the small fibrous tuft near the hinge) by pulling them sharply downward or cutting them away. Gently squeeze the shell; if it does not close tightly, discard the mussel. Also, discard any mussels that are particularly heavy, as they may be full of sand.

In a large, tall pot over high heat, warm the oil. Add the garlic and shallot and sauté until fragrant, about 1 minute. Add the wine and hot pepper sauce, bring to a boil, and cook for 2 minutes to blend the flavors. Add the parsley, thyme, salt, and mussels and cover tightly. Cook over high heat, shaking the pot once or twice, until most of the mussels have opened, 3–4 minutes. The pot can sometimes boil over, so watch carefully and lift the lid for a few seconds once or twice during cooking. Using a slotted spoon, transfer the open mussels to a large bowl. Re-cover and continue to cook for 1 minute until the remaining mussels open, then transfer them to the bowl. Discard any mussels that have not opened.

Divide the mussels among individual bowls, or leave them in the large bowl. Ladle the cooking broth over them and serve right away.

MAKES 4 SERVINGS

4 lb mussels, debearded and scrubbed clean

2 tbsp extra-virgin olive oil

2 large cloves garlic, finely chopped

1 shallot, finely chopped

1/2 cup dry soft white wine

2 or 3 dashes hot red pepper sauce such as Tabasco

1/3 cup chopped fresh flat-leaf parsley

2 fresh thyme sprigs

1/4 tsp kosher salt

New World match

The ripe fruit of an Oregon Pinot Gris complements the sweet meat of the mussels.

Old World matches

A stony Austrian Grüner Veltliner will emphasize the minerality in both the shellfish and the wine-based steaming liquid.

For a slightly richer expression of flavors, choose an Alsatian Pinot Blanc.

Alternative pairing

For a lighter, bubbly partner, try a dry German Sekt (Sparkling Wines, page 38).

Braised chicken thighs with orange & star anise

A medium-bodied wine corresponds to the texture of this dish. Choose one that's slightly off-dry to match the sweetness of the orange and contrast with the salty and spicy elements.

8 skin-on, bone-in chicken thighs

Kosher salt and freshly ground black pepper

2 tbsp peanut oil

1/2 cup finely chopped yellow onion

2 cloves garlic, minced

1 tsp peeled and grated fresh ginger

Grated zest of 1 orange

1/2 cup fresh orange juice

1/3 cup reduced-sodium chicken broth

1 tbsp soy sauce

2 tsp Sriracha sauce

2 whole star anise

1 tsp cornstarch dissolved in 1 tbsp cold water

2 cups hot cooked white rice for serving

Season the chicken thighs on both sides with salt and pepper. In a large frying pan over medium-high heat, warm the oil. Working in batches if necessary to avoid crowding, add the chicken thighs, skin side down, to the hot oil and cook until the skin is nicely browned, 6–8 minutes. Turn the chicken pieces over and cook until lightly browned on the second side, 3–4 minutes longer. Transfer the chicken to a plate and let cool slightly. When cool enough to handle, pull off and discard the skin.

Pour off all but 1 tablespoon of the fat from the pan and return the pan to medium heat. Add the onion and sauté until translucent and soft, 3–4 minutes. Add the garlic, ginger, and orange zest and sauté until fragrant, 1–2 minutes. Pour in the orange juice, broth, soy sauce, and Sriracha sauce and stir to mix. Return the chicken pieces to the pan, add the star anise, and bring the mixture to a boil. Reduce the heat to low, cover, and simmer until the chicken is opaque throughout when tested with a knife tip, about 25 minutes.

Remove the star anise from the cooking liquid and discard. Transfer the chicken to a warmed serving dish. Bring the liquid in the pan to a boil over medium-high heat, stir in the cornstarch mixture, and cook, stirring, until the sauce thickens, 1–2 minutes.

Pour the pan sauce over the chicken. Serve right away with the rice.

MAKES 4 SERVINGS

New World matches

To handle the sweet-and-sour flavors, pick an off-dry Riesling from New York's Finger Lakes.

A Chenin Blanc from California's North Coast brings a rounder set of flavors and textures to flatter the dish.

Old World match

Riesling purists can complement this dish with a German wine from the Mosel.

Alternative pairing

Pour an Anjou Rosé (Pink Wines, page 99) for its cherry-kissed fruit and modest alcohol.

Pork tenderloin with apple & onion compote

Here, the firm, juicy texture of pork tenderloin forms a textural match with the wine. The fruity compote reinforces the link, complementing similar flavors in the wine.

2 pork tenderloins,
1–1¼ lb each, trimmed

Kosher salt and freshly ground black pepper

2 tbsp apple jelly

2 tbsp Dijon mustard

COMPOTE
2 tbsp unsalted butter

1 large yellow onion, quartered lengthwise and thinly sliced crosswise

¼ tsp kosher salt

2 Granny Smith or other tart green apples, peeled and cut into ¼-inch cubes

⅓ cup golden raisins

2 tbsp apple jelly

1 tsp peeled and grated fresh ginger

½ tsp dry mustard

4 drops hot red pepper sauce such as Tabasco

Dash of ground white pepper

½ cup dry Riesling or other soft white wine

Preheat the oven to 425°F. Line a roasting pan with aluminum foil. Oil a rack large enough to hold the tenderloins and place the rack in the pan.

Generously season the tenderloins with salt and black pepper. In a small bowl, whisk together the apple jelly and mustard. Brush the mixture on all sides of the tenderloins, and place the tenderloins on the rack. Roast until an instant-read thermometer inserted into the thickest part of a tenderloin registers 145°–150°F or until the meat is a pale pink at the center when tested with a knife, 30–35 minutes. Transfer the tenderloins to a platter, lightly tent with aluminum foil, and let rest for 10 minutes.

While the pork is roasting, make the compote. In a frying pan over medium heat, melt the butter. Add the onion and salt and sauté until the onion is lightly golden, 8–10 minutes. Add the apples, raisins, apple jelly, ginger, mustard, hot-pepper sauce, and white pepper and stir to combine. Pour in the wine, bring to a boil, then reduce the heat to low, cover, and simmer, stirring occasionally, until the apples are soft, about 10 minutes. If the mixture is too thin, uncover and continue to cook for a few minutes until it has reduced and thickened. Transfer the compote to a serving bowl and serve warm or at room temperature.

To serve, cut the tenderloins on the diagonal into slices ½ inch thick and season with salt. Spoon the compote onto warmed individual plates and arrange the pork slices on top.

MAKES 4–6 SERVINGS

New World match

Choose an Oregon Pinot Gris for a medium-bodied, richly flavored wine to flatter the dish's sweet and savory tastes.

Old World match

The full flavors of an Alsatian Gewürztraminer will richly echo those on the plate.

To add refinement with the same relative flavor profile, serve a Rheingau *Halbtrocken* Riesling.

Alternative pairing

A New Zealand Pinot Noir (Juicy Reds, page 112) will echo the fruit and accent the savory pork.

Rich whites

Creamy, full flavored, and luxurious, rich whites feature an array of fruit aromas, a dash of oak, and a buttery mouthfeel. These opulent wines are perfect companions to equally lavish foods.

Rich whites are characterized by their concentrated flavors and complexity. Chardonnay is by far the top grape in this category, but Viognier, Chardonnay's exotic cousin, has gained popularity, as have other regional grapes throughout the world. Oak figures prominently in this wine style, lending its smoky, toasty flavors and structure to the wines. Rich whites match well with foods that have the same relative fullness or are enhanced by the wines' wide range of fruit flavors—from tart apples to citrus to tropical fruits. Some heavily oaked wines of this style, more common in the New World than the old, need special consideration when pairing them with a meal.

About rich whites

An array of fruity aromas; full, layered flavors; and a creamy texture distinguish the rich white category. Often these wines spend time in oak barrels, which adds additional weight to the wine as well as pronounced vanilla or nut aromas. Because they are so heavy on the palate, rich whites are typically better enjoyed with food than on their own. That way, the wine can be balanced by full-flavored ingredients.

Oak influence in wine

Fermenting or aging wines in oak barrels for various periods of time tends to soften the wine and add to its richness; it is a common practice for rich whites and a number of red wines. The wood also imparts some of its characteristic flavors and tannins. Barrel aging is a common practice of California and Australian producers of Chardonnay, as drinkers in those markets enjoy a pronounced oak flavor and creamy quality in their wine. That said, too much oak can overpower the wine and make it difficult to match to food.

Attributes of rich whites

The best rich whites have lively acidity to offset their lushness; such well-balanced wines will also pair better with food. Richly flavored or textured food is the best match here, but dishes that are too complex can compete with the layered flavors of the wine. Rich whites can be a bit more expensive than other white wine styles, so it makes sense to serve them on special occasions when you would typically serve richer foods.

A buttery wine is a natural match for foods topped with a butter- or cream-based sauce. Rich, meaty fish and shellfish, such as crab, lobster, and scallops, are also natural partners, as their dense texture and opulent flavors match that of the wine. The cooking method employed in the recipe can also help form the a match with a rich white. For example, the smoky flavors of chicken or fish cooked on a grill will echo similar flavors in an oak-aged wine. The full, rich texture imparted by braising foods helps match the wine's round mouthfeel. Foods with bolder, more exotic flavors often do better with full-bodied whites that feature spice, honey, or stone-fruit aromas. To reinforce these matches, pair the foods with companion ingredients that have the same relative flavors as the wine. Avoid pairing rich whites with very spicy dishes, which will highlight the alcohol and oak in the wine, rather than the other flavors.

1 Look

Rich whites range in color from light yellow to rich gold. This deep shade is due partly to rich whites' tendency to be found in warmer climates, and also because these wines are frequently aged in oak, both of which contribute to a darker-hued wine.

2 Swirl

Rich whites tend to be the highest in alcohol of all the white wine styles. This will cause a wine's legs to remain for a time on the side of the glass after you swirl it. The wine may also appear slightly thick. Be sure to swirl the wine briskly to release its complex aromas.

3 Smell

There is a wide variety of fruit aromas, characteristic of the individual grapes, in rich whites. You may also notice some toasty, nutty scents, which indicate the wine has been aged in oak.

4 Sip

Beyond the distinctive flavors of the grapes themselves, what will be most noticeable is the way a rich white fills and coats your mouth. Some describe this round, viscous feeling as "oily." If accompanied by enough acidity, the result should be a nicely balanced wine. Rich whites typically have long finishes compared to other white wine styles.

Flavor profile

Rich whites from the Old World feature tangy fruit aromas laced with light scents of vanilla and toasted nuts, which come from brief contact with oak. Rich whites from the New World tend to be more hard-hitting, both in their fruity aromas—leaning more toward tropical fruits—and the pronounced smoky or toasty aromas from the heavier use of oak in the maturing process.

Peach

The aroma and flavor of both Chardonnay and Viognier often feature undertones of fresh ripe peaches.

Vanilla

Like toast and nuts, a vanilla flavor comes from aging a wine in oak, a common practice in rich whites.

Toast

A toasty aroma is the influence of the oak barrels on the wine. When subtle, it is a desirable trait in rich whites. In excess, a toasty wine is difficult to match to food.

Butter

Chardonnay, especially in the New World, is often described as buttery, reflecting its color, flavor, and mouth-coating texture.

Pear

Many rich whites smell and taste of soft, honeyed tree fruits such as ripe pears.

Herbs

An herbal scent in a rich white is common in both oak-aged Sauvignon Blancs and wines from France's Rhône Valley, where herbs grow wild near the vineyards.

Mango

Rich whites from the New World are often described as having tropical fruit aromas and flavors, such as from a fresh mango.

Cream

The impression of creaminess is more a texture than a flavor, and distinguishes rich whites from other types of white wines.

Hazelnut

The nutty characteristics in many rich whites come from aging the wine in toasted oak barrels.

Orange

Orange and other citrus aromas and flavors create an acidic backbone for a number of rich white wines.

Key rich white wines

Of all the white wine styles, rich whites have the best aging potential, in part because of structure added from fermenting or aging in oak barrels. For the most successful food and wine matches, avoid labels that indicate a wine has spent more than 12 months in oak; these can be tricky to match. Rich whites show best when they are not ice cold, which can mask their complexity.

Malolactic fermentation

Malic acid, with the flavor of green apples, is a naturally occurring substance in grapes, but some consider it to be rather harsh. Malic acid can be converted to softer lactic acid through a process called *malolactic fermentation,* which can happen spontaneously or be induced through the introduction of bacteria. In the production of white wines, commonly in Chardonnay, winemakers make a conscious choice to encourage or generate this process, depending on whether they prefer a wine in a light and crisp or a round and lush style.

Chardonnay

The aromas of Chardonnay are diverse. Some wines smell of apples, melons, and ripe pears, while others are reminiscent of tropical fruits such as mangoes, bananas, and papayas. Considered one of the world's great wine grapes, Chardonnay is responsible for the white Burgundies of France. There it forms wines of great complexity, with subtle oak flavors. All over the world, winemakers are emulating Burgundy's fine tradition. California is perhaps the most famous, notably Napa and Sonoma, but Chardonnay is also widely planted in Australia, Chile, and South Africa, among other New World regions. Although distinct regional styles of Chardonnay do exist, it can be difficult to establish them, since Chardonnay is easily manipulated by the winemaker and the use of oak—typically more pronounced in New World wines than in Old World wines—has a profound effect on the wine. Chardonnay is used to make two other distinctively different wines: It is a primary grape in Champagne and Champagne-style wines (see Sparkling Wines, page 38), and can be found in an acidic, unoaked style (see Crisp Whites, page 53).

Viognier

Not very long ago, Viognier was grown only in a small area in France's Rhône valley, where it made a lovely but relatively unknown wine called Condrieu, scented with peaches, apricots, and honeysuckle. Today, Viognier's popularity has expanded to cult status, rivaling even that of Chardonnay in some circles. Although the worldwide production of Viognier is still relatively low, to meet the ever-increasing demand there has been an upsurge in production in Viognier plantings elsewhere in France, as well as California, Oregon, Washington, and Virginia in the United States; Tuscany, in Italy; and Austria. Viognier makes a distinctive wine with delicate aromas and flavors of ripe apricot and pear, featuring an intriguing honeyed finish, even though the wine is dry. With all its fascinating aromas, Viognier could almost be considered a soft white, but for its buttery mouthfeel and relatively high alcohol content. Like Chardonnay, it is common to have significant oak influence in Viognier. But unlike Chardonnay, Viognier can be paired successfully with complex ethnic dishes that are heavily seasoned.

Sauvignon Blanc

Usually made as a crisp white (page 52), Sauvignon Blanc can also be made in a richer style by aging the wine in oak barrels, lending a fuller flavor and body to the naturally light wine. This richer style is common in France's Bordeaux region, particularly in Graves, where it is sometimes blended with Semillon to further enhance the wine's complexity. In the U.S., oak-aging Sauvignon Blanc is popular in California. There, the wine is sometimes labeled Fumé Blanc.

White Rioja

Macabeo, also called Viura, is the major grape of white wines from the Rioja region of Spain. Aged extensively in oak, these wines take on a rich, mouth-filling quality and toasty flavors. Look for the words "Reserva" or "Gran Reserva" on the wine labels for the fullest flavor and texture. Macabeo is also used in blends for table wine in other parts of Spain and Southwest France. The same wine can also be made in a youthful style (see Crisp Whites, page 53).

Semillon

Consider Semillon the "buddy grape," as it is usually found blended with Sauvignon Blanc, especially in Bordeaux, France, and with Chardonnay in Australia and in California. Australia and Washington State produce some full-varietal Semillons, redolent of tropical fruits with a spicy, toasty background. Semillon also makes some of the world's top dessert wines (see Sweet Whites, page 156).

Marsanne

Marsanne is seen mostly in the Rhône region of France, where it is often blended with Rousanne and other grapes. Marsanne is also widely grown in Australia, where it makes wines with a rich, nutty character.

Roussane

Rousanne makes perfumed, elegant white wines, which are at their best in France's Rhône valley, where it is often blended with Marsanne. It is also used to make Châteauneuf-du-Pape Blanc, a rare but delicious find.

White wine & meat

In old food-and-wine-pairing rules, red wine was the only type of wine to serve with meat. But meat can be served successfully with white wine if you are careful with the match. Choose mild meats such as pork or veal and pair them with complementary companion ingredients: cream sauces, tropical fruit relishes, or nut crusts all work well. Red meats, too, can be paired with white wines if they are cooked for a long time, such as in a braised preparation. For best results, pair meats with a rich white, which has a complementary texture.

Seared scallops with curried pea sauce

Rich scallops coupled with puréed peas match the full texture of this wine style, while meaty prosciutto strengthens the link to the wine. The exotic spices bring out a wine's oak flavor.

2 tbsp unsalted butter

1/2 cup finely chopped yellow onion

1 small clove garlic, minced

1 tsp curry powder

2 cups fresh or thawed, frozen shelled English peas

1 cup reduced-sodium chicken broth

Kosher salt and freshly ground pepper

9 thin slices prosciutto, about 1/4 lb total weight, cut in half lengthwise

18 large scallops, about 1 lb total weight, tough side muscle removed

1 tsp extra-virgin olive oil

Chopped fresh mint leaves for garnish

In a saucepan over medium-low heat, melt the butter. Add the onion and garlic and sauté until the onion is soft and translucent, about 5 minutes. Do not allow the onion to color. Add the curry powder and cook, stirring, until fragrant, 1–2 minutes. Stir in the peas and broth. Bring to a boil over high heat. Reduce the heat to low, and simmer, uncovered, until the peas are soft, about 10 minutes. Remove from the heat and let stand for 5–10 minutes to cool slightly.

Ladle half of the peas and broth into a blender, and process on high speed until very smooth. Pour the purée through a medium-mesh sieve into a bowl. Process the remaining peas and broth in the blender until very smooth, and pour through the sieve. Using the back of the ladle, press firmly against the purée, forcing as much through as possible. Discard the contents of sieve. There should be about 1 1/2 cups sauce. Season to taste with salt and pepper; set aside.

Trim each prosciutto strip as necessary to match the thickness of the scallops. Wrap 1 strip of prosciutto around the side of each scallop, overlapping the ends, and secure with a toothpick.

Heat a large nonstick frying pan over medium-high heat until very hot. Add the oil and heat until very hot. Add the scallops and sear, turning once, until lightly browned on both sides and just opaque in the center, 1–2 minutes on each side. Remove from the heat. In a clean saucepan over low heat, warm the sauce until heated through. Divide the hot sauce among warmed individual plates and place 3 scallops on each pool of sauce. Garnish with the mint and serve right away.

MAKES 6 FIRST-COURSE SERVINGS

New World matches

The "green" flavors of a Napa Fumé Blanc will reference both the richness of the scallops and the vegetal peas.

The slightly herbal character of a Semillon from Washington State will shadow the minty pea purée.

Old World match

Seek out a Condrieu from the northern Rhône, whose Viognier base will highlight the scallops' natural sweetness.

Alternative pairing

A cleansing Vouvray *mousseux* (Sparkling Wines, page 39) will echo the implied sweetness in the dish.

Fresh corn soup with shiitake mushrooms

Creamy and nutty, fresh corn has a natural affinity to oak-aged wines. Rich chicken broth helps create a textural balance in the soup, while earthy mushrooms create a link to the wine's *terroir*.

Break the corn cobs in half, place in a large saucepan with the bay leaf, and add water just to cover. Bring to a boil over high heat, reduce the heat to low, and simmer, uncovered, for 15 minutes. Strain the corn broth, discarding the cobs and bay leaf. Measure out 2 cups of the broth and discard the remainder.

In a heavy saucepan over medium heat, melt the 2 tablespoons butter. Add the onion and celery and sauté until the onion is translucent, about 10 minutes. Add the garlic and cook, stirring, until fragrant, about 1 minute. Add the reserved corn kernels, the 2 cups corn broth, the chicken broth, sugar, salt, and cayenne pepper. Bring to a boil over high heat. Reduce the heat to low and simmer until all the vegetables are tender, 10–15 minutes.

Remove from the heat and let stand for about 10 minutes to cool slightly. Working in small batches, ladle the soup into a blender and process until very smooth. As each batch is puréed, pour it through a medium-mesh sieve into a clean saucepan, forcing as much through as possible with the back of the ladle. Discard the pulp in the sieve. Reheat the soup over low heat until warmed through.

Meanwhile, in a small frying pan over medium-high heat, melt the remaining 1 teaspoon butter. Add the mushrooms and sauté them until they release their moisture and are lightly browned, 2–3 minutes. Add the vinegar and cook for another 30 seconds. Remove from the heat.

Ladle the soup into warmed bowls or cups. Garnish with the mushrooms and serve right away.

MAKES 6 SERVINGS

Ingredients

5 ears fresh corn, shucked, kernels removed, and cobs reserved

1 bay leaf

2 tbsp plus 1 tsp unsalted butter

1 medium yellow onion, thinly sliced

1 celery stalk, finely chopped

2 cloves garlic, minced

1¾ cups reduced-sodium chicken broth

½ tsp sugar

½ tsp kosher salt

Pinch of cayenne pepper or ground white pepper

8–10 fresh small shiitake mushrooms, about 2 oz total weight, brushed clean, stems discarded, and cut into ½-inch pieces

1 tsp sherry vinegar

New World matches

An oak-aged Napa or Sonoma Chardonnay will match the soup's creamy-sweet richness.

Similarly, an oak-aged Chardonnay from South Australia will reflect both the nuttiness and earthiness of the soup.

Old World match

To play up the corn's natural sweetness, try a Puligny Montrachet from Burgundy.

Alternative pairing

For both contrasting and complementary flavors and textures, choose a nonvintage Brut Champagne (Sparkling Wines, page 38).

Salmon roulades with pesto & crème fraîche

The oily fish, luscious crème fraîche, and rustic texture of the pesto create a tactile link with the full-bodied wine. Toasting the nuts for the pesto echoes the wine's oak flavors.

1 cup firmly packed fresh basil leaves

1/3 cup slivered blanched almonds, toasted

2 cloves garlic

1/3 cup plus 2 tbsp extra-virgin olive oil

Kosher salt

1/2 cup crème fraîche

1 tsp grated lemon zest

1 tbsp fresh lemon juice

4 salmon steaks, each 6–8 oz and 3/4 inch thick

2 tbsp all-purpose flour

Freshly ground pepper

Roughly chopped fresh basil leaves, for garnish

To make the pesto, in a food processor, combine the basil, almonds, garlic, 1/3 cup of the olive oil, and 1/2 teaspoon salt. Pulse several times to mix and then process until well chopped, stopping to scrape down the sides of the bowl as needed. Measure out 5 tablespoons of the pesto and set aside. Reserve the remaining pesto for another use; cover it tightly and refrigerate for up to 2 days.

In a bowl, whisk together the crème fraîche, the 5 tablespoons pesto, and the lemon zest and juice. Refrigerate until ready to serve.

Using a small, sharp knife, remove the skin from the salmon steaks. Cut along both sides of the bone in each steak and separate the steak into halves. Check for small bones by running your fingers over the salmon pieces, and pull out any you find with your fingers or fish tweezers. Turn each steak half over, and then position the halves so that the narrow end of one-half wraps around the larger end of the other half to form a pinwheel, or roulade. Use toothpicks to secure the small ends and hold the roulade together.

Spread the flour on a large, shallow plate. Lightly season both sides of each roulade with salt and pepper, and lightly dust both sides with the flour. In a large frying pan over medium-high heat, warm the remaining 2 tablespoons oil. Add the roulades and cook, turning once about halfway through cooking, until both sides are firm to the touch and the centers are just barely pink when tested with a knife tip, 6–8 minutes total.

Transfer the roulades to warmed individual plates and remove the toothpicks. Place a spoonful of sauce alongside. Garnish with the basil and serve right away.

MAKES 4 SERVINGS

New World match

For its light oak and citrus flavors, choose a Central Coast blend of Roussane and Marsanne.

Old World match

A white Graves from Bordeaux has both the richness and acidity to handle the multiple tastes and textures here.

Alternative pairings

A Pinot Gris from New Zealand (Soft Whites, page 69) will offer complementary flavors without any oak.

The bright fruit and fine acidity of a Clare Valley Australian Riesling (Soft Whites, page 68) will contrast the rich flavors.

Lobster risotto

The richness of the ingredients here is matched by a full-bodied wine. The wine's acid, coupled with the lemon and tomato in the dish, will prevent the pair from overwhelming.

3 cups reduced-sodium chicken broth

3 tbsp extra-virgin olive oil

$\frac{1}{2}$ cup finely chopped yellow onion

Pinch of red pepper flakes

1 cup Arborio rice

$\frac{1}{4}$ cup rich white wine

$\frac{1}{2}$ tsp grated lemon zest

1 tbsp fresh lemon juice

Pinch of saffron threads, optional

$\frac{1}{2}$ tsp kosher salt

$\frac{1}{2}$ lb cooked lobster tail meat, coarsely chopped

$\frac{1}{2}$ cup peeled, seeded, and finely chopped tomato

2 tbsp unsalted butter

Pour the broth into a small saucepan, bring to a simmer over medium heat, and adjust the heat to keep the broth at a bare simmer. In a large, heavy saucepan over medium-low heat, warm the oil. Add the onion and red pepper flakes and sauté until the onion is soft, about 3–4 minutes. Add the rice and cook, stirring to coat it with the onion mixture, until the grains are opaque, about 2 minutes. Add the wine, lemon zest and juice, and saffron threads, if using, and cook for 2 minutes.

Add the salt to the simmering broth, and then begin adding the hot broth to the rice $\frac{1}{2}$ cup at a time, stirring often and waiting until each addition is almost fully absorbed before adding more. After about 20 minutes, when you have added all but $\frac{1}{2}$ cup of the broth, the mixture should look creamy. Taste a grain of rice: it should be cooked through but still be slightly firm—not hard—at the center. If it is still too firm, add the remaining broth and continue cooking.

When the rice is ready, stir in the lobster, distributing it evenly, and then stir in the tomato and butter. Taste and adjust the seasonings, remove from the heat, and let stand, covered, for 5 minutes before serving to heat through the lobster and tomato.

Spoon the risotto into warmed shallow bowls and serve right away.

MAKES 6–8 FIRST-COURSE SERVINGS, OR 4 MAIN-COURSE SERVINGS

New World match

The rich flavors and creamy texture of an Australian Semillon will nicely complement this indulgent risotto.

Old World match

Try a Pouilly-Fuissé from Burgundy, whose roundness but relative modesty will highlight the risotto's rich flavors.

Alternative pairings

The bubbles of a Brut Champagne (Sparkling Wines, page 38) will cut the dish's richness and enhance the lobster.

A fruity, mineral-tinged Albariño (Crisp Whites, page 53) will flatter the seafood while cutting the dish's creaminess.

Roast chicken with mustard cream sauce

Butter, cream, and crisp chicken skin call for a full-bodied wine; choose one with bright acidity to cut through the richness. Mustard and garlic are flavorful bridges linking the elements.

1 chicken, 4–4½ lb, giblets and neck removed and reserved for another use, if desired

2 tbsp Dijon mustard

2 tsp extra-virgin olive oil

3 tbsp chopped fresh tarragon, plus 1 sprig

Kosher salt and freshly ground pepper

3 or 4 cloves garlic, peeled but left whole

1¾ cups reduced-sodium chicken broth

3 tbsp unsalted butter

3 tbsp all-purpose flour

⅓ cup heavy cream

Preheat the oven to 400°F. Use your fingers to gently separate the skin from the meat on the breast, thighs, and drumsticks. In a small bowl, stir together 1 tablespoon of the mustard, 1 teaspoon of the oil, 1 tablespoon of the chopped tarragon, and several generous grinds of black pepper. Carefully push this mixture under the skin, distributing it evenly over the meat. Season the cavity with salt and pepper, and add the tarragon sprig and garlic. Rub the remaining 1 teaspoon oil evenly over the bird and season with salt and pepper. Place the chicken breast side up on an oiled roasting rack in a roasting pan. Roast until an instant-read thermometer inserted into the thickest part of the thigh away from bone registers 170°–175°F, about 1 hour. Transfer the chicken to a carving board, lightly tent with aluminum foil, and let rest for 15 minutes.

Meanwhile, remove the rack from the roasting pan and place the pan over low heat. Pour in the broth and bring to a simmer, scraping up the browned bits from the pan bottom, for 2–3 minutes. Pour the liquid from the pan through a fine-mesh sieve into a glass measuring cup. Using a large spoon, skim the fat from the top of the liquid and discard. In a saucepan over medium heat, melt the butter. Whisk in the flour and cook, stirring, until the mixture turns golden, 2–3 minutes. Gradually add the broth mixture, whisking constantly. Whisk in the remaining 1 tablespoon mustard, the remaining 2 tablespoons tarragon, ¼ teaspoon salt, and ¼ teaspoon pepper. Bring the sauce to a boil over high heat, reduce the heat to low, and simmer, stirring occasionally, until slightly thickened, about 10 minutes. Stir in the cream and heat through.

Carve the chicken into serving pieces and divide among warmed plates. Spoon a little of the sauce over the chicken pieces and serve right away.

MAKES 4 SERVINGS

New World match

A Chardonnay from the Central Coast of California will have both the depth of flavor and vital acidity to handle the dish's rich elements.

Old World match

Choose a Burgundy from St. Veran for a French-accented match with this bistro-style chicken dish.

Alternative pairings

The bright fruit and acidic tang of a Cru Beaujolais (Juicy Reds, page 112) will nicely contrast with the dish.

With its low tannins and acidity, a rosé of Pinot Noir (Pink Wines, page 98) will form similar pleasing contrasts.

Pork chops braised with garlic & white beans

Braising gives the chops additional weight, helping them match a full-bodied wine. Meaty white beans provide another textural element, and nutty, slow-cooked garlic brings out oak flavors.

4 center-cut pork chops, each 8–10 oz and about 1 inch thick

Kosher salt and freshly ground black pepper

3 tbsp extra-virgin olive oil

1 large yellow onion, finely chopped

2 carrots, peeled and finely chopped

1 head garlic, separated into cloves and peeled (about 12 cloves)

¼ tsp red pepper flakes, or to taste

3 or 4 fresh sage leaves

1¾ cups reduced-sodium chicken broth

2 cans white beans, drained and rinsed

¼ cup chopped fresh flat-leaf parsley

Preheat the oven to 350°F.

Season the pork chops on both sides with salt and pepper. In a Dutch oven, heat the oil over medium-high heat Add the chops and sear, turning once, until nicely browned on both sides, 6–8 minutes total. Transfer the pork chops to a platter.

Reduce the heat to medium-low, add the onion, carrots, garlic, and red pepper flakes, and stir well, scraping up the browned bits on the pan bottom. Sauté until the vegetables are soft, 3–4 minutes. Add the sage leaves and broth and bring to a boil over high heat, then remove from the heat. Return the pork chops to the pan, cover, transfer the pan to the oven, and braise for 20 minutes.

Meanwhile, place half of the white beans in a small bowl and use a fork to coarsely mash them. When the chops have cooked for 20 minutes, add both the mashed and whole beans to the pot and continue to cook, uncovered, until the pork chops are tender and the sauce has thickened slightly, about 15 minutes longer.

Divide the sauce among warmed shallow bowls and top with the pork chops. Spoon a little more sauce over the top. Garnish with the parsley and serve right away.

MAKES 4 SERVINGS

New World match

With its rich, barrel-aged flavors, an oaked white Rioja will take on all the flavors in this seriously meaty dish.

Old World match

A Côtes-du-Rhône Blanc, including Marsanne, Roussanne, and Viognier, will be rich enough to stand up to the pork.

Alternative pairings

Choose a Grenache-based rosé (Pink Wines, page 98) to highlight the almost-sweet braised flavors in the sauce.

These pork chops will taste even meatier with a peppery Côtes-du-Rhône Rouge (Juicy Reds, page 113).

Pink wines

Brisk, succulent, and unfussy, pink wines—or rosés—are bursting with red fruit flavors. They are versatile wines, pairing with a variety of foods, especially when serving them al fresco.

By many accounts, the best examples of rosés come from the south of France and northern Spain; there they are presented as dry wines, often based on the Grenache grape, which lends its lemony, peppery flavors to the crisp, refreshing wines. Pink wines can be made from a wide variety of red grapes, such as Syrah, Pinot Noir, and Cabernet Sauvignon. Even in the United States, where some consider "blush" wines to be unsophisticated or too sweet, winemakers are responding to an increased demand for the true style of dry rosé discovered by well-traveled wine drinkers. Rosés are excellent food wines and are especially suited to dishes featuring bold Mediterranean flavors.

About pink wines

Pink wines, or rosés, have all the food-friendly acidity of crisp whites (see page 49) coupled with the cherry-berry flavors of juicy reds (see page 109). Rosés fall on the light end of the wine body spectrum, but they can vary substantially in style within that range. Some are racy and crisp while others are rich and full. Having qualities of both whites and reds, pink wines pair well with an array of different foods.

Vin gris

Literally "gray wine" in French, *vin gris* traditionally refers to very pale rosé wines, which are made by leaving the grape juice in contact with the red skins for a very short period of time. This process makes light-bodied, fresh-tasting wines, meant to be consumed as soon as they are bottled. In the U.S. the term "vin gris" is fashionable on a wide range of rosés, even some in fuller-bodied styles and with deep pink hues.

Attributes of pink wines

Rosés start as red wines do, except that the fermenting juice is kept in contact with the grape skins for a much shorter period of time than a fully red wine. This process allows some color to be extracted from the skins, but very little of the tannin that is associated with red wines made from the same grapes. Pink wines are all about fruit, so you want to drink them while they are young (fruit flavors dissipate as wines age). Lighter-bodied rosés are aged in stainless-steel vats, which protects their pronounced fruit flavors. Fuller-bodied rosés are sometimes aged in neutral oak barrels, which lends body and structure, but not much flavor, to the wine.

Rosés are ubiquitous table wines in Southern Europe, where they pair effortlessly with the foods of the region, such as pissaladière, paella, or Mediterranean fish stew. It's typical to see more rosés in the summertime than the winter, and they are served well chilled to highlight their refreshing qualities. As with crisp whites, rosés' bracing acidity acts like a lemon squeeze for food, highlighting a dish's flavors. Rosés can also stand up to sour or salty ingredients (such as capers, cornichons, and salad dressings) or heavily spiced ethnic dishes (such as Mexican or Moroccan cuisines) that would fight with less acidic wines. Pink wines are wonderful paired with charcuterie or pâté, where their acid cuts through the food's richness.

1 Look

Rosés are found in a dazzling array of colors, from light salmon to deep pink. The hue is dictated both by the color of the grape skins and how long the skins stay in contact with the wine. A lighter color doesn't necessarily mean an inferior wine.

2 Swirl

Young and light, rosés will look thin in the glass. The legs will not be pronounced and will disappear rapidly. If you are sampling a sparkling rosé, you don't need to swirl it. Look for a strong stream of bubbles, ideally on the small side.

3 Smell

When you smell a pink wine, red fruit—whether cherries or berries—will be the primary aroma that you detect. Citrus, fresh-cut flowers, and stones are also typical scents.

4 Sip

As with a crisp white, a sip of a pink wine will reveal a bracing acidity. Here, though, it is layered with pronounced cherry and berry flavors. A darker rosé may be slightly more astringent than a lighter one, as it has been in contact with the grape skins for a longer period of time. Regardless of style, a good rosé will be dry, which may be obscured slightly by the wine's intense fruitiness.

Flavor profile

In general, Old World rosés have clean, zesty flavors and mineral accents. Their alcohol content may be on the low side, in keeping with the light-bodied style common to the region. By contrast, in the New World, the grapes are likely to be grown in hotter climates where both their fruit flavors and alcohol content are enhanced. Here, the wines tend to boast a fuller, creamier style.

Cherry

Cherry-scented wines are prevalent throughout the pink wine category, coupled with other red fruit flavors.

Dried cherry

Pink wines from warmer climates tend to show more concentrated cherry flavors, more like dried cherries than fresh.

Raspberry

Fresh raspberries, even raspberry jam, are typical descriptions of the flavors in pink wines.

Grapefruit

The bracing flavor of grapefruit forms a refreshing core for a variety of pink wines.

Floral

A wide range of floral scents can be perceived in pink wines, such as orange blossoms, roses, and flowering lavender.

Strawberry

Jammy strawberry flavors are prominent in many types of pink wines, from both the Old and New World wine regions.

Pomegranate

Tart and slightly astringent, a flavor reminiscent of pomegranate is common in rosés that have had lengthy contact with the grape skins.

Cranberry

The fresh flavor and bright acidity of many types of rosé reminds tasters of naturally tart fresh cranberries.

Mineral

The mineral-rich soil of many Old World vineyards contributes its flavor to a variety of rosés, lending a clean finish to the wines.

Quince

The perfumed aroma of fresh quince comes through in many rosés, particularly those made from Pinot Noir.

Key pink wines

Rosés are made to be drunk young to appreciate their fresh qualities, so look for a recent vintage on the store shelf. Lighter-style rosés will tend to have a lower alcohol content, heavier-style rosés a higher percentage. Fuller styles will also tend to have a darker, more saturated hue, but this is not a hard-and-fast rule. Experiment with the wide range of rosés on the market to discover your favorites.

Blush wines

The term "blush" was invented as a marketing strategy in California in the 1980s. The marketers were looking to distance themselves from the term "rosé," as it had been associated in the United States with cheap pink jug wines. The star performer under the blush wine banner became White Zinfandel, a simple, light, slightly sweet wine. Although a few winemakers make delicious dry rosés from the Zinfandel grape, most White Zinfandel—still very popular in the U.S.— is a far cry from the dry, food-friendly rosés based on Old World traditions.

Grenache

This grape thrives in hot weather, notably in southern France and Spain. Because of the warm climate, the grapes tend to get very ripe, leading to rosés with bright fruit and a relatively full mouthfeel. In France, Grenache is the primary grape in wines from Tavel, arguably the most famous rosé region in the world. Tavel rosés can be somewhat high in alcohol and are on the full-bodied end of the spectrum for rosés. For that reason they are among the few pink wines that have any aging potential; most rosés should be consumed as soon as they are purchased. Grenache also forms the basis for dozens of other wines in Provence, including the widely available Côtes de Provence. Adjacent to Provence in the Languedoc region, Grenache also figures in the local rosés, often blended with Carignane. In Spain, where the rosés are called *rosados* and the grape is called Garnacha, the grape is also common, making pleasingly rustic pink wines in the Rioja and Navarra regions. In the New World, California produces many fine examples of European-style dry rosés made from Grenache or blended with Syrah, Mourvèdre, and other grapes reminiscent of those popular in Northern Provence.

Syrah

Syrah is a typical grape in many of the rosés of the southern Rhône and Provence, and it's usually blended with Grenache, Mourvèdre, and other local grapes. Syrah is also made as a single-varietal rosé in a fruit-forward New World style in France's Languedoc region. Many wineries specializing in Rhône-style wines in central and Northern California also make rosé from Syrah grapes. Syrah rosé is also made in Australia. While the typical barnyard aromas of the grape do not show in a rosé, the wine is still full flavored and imbued with spice.

Pinot Noir

In the Old World, Pinot Noir is made into refined, fruity rosés from Burgundy, France, particularly in the Marsennay region, as well as brisk, low-alcohol pink wines from the Sancerre region in the Loire Valley. In the New World, California produces elegant Pinot Noir rosés in Napa, Sonoma, Santa Barbara, and other areas famous for Pinot Noir–based reds.

Merlot

Dry rosés made from the soft Merlot grape are common to the Bordeaux region of France and they are also now being made in California a single varietal rosés and in blends. Pass up the sweetish blush wine labeled "White Merlot," which will taste closer to White Zinfandel (see left) than a European-style dry rosé.

Sangiovese

In California, New World winemakers are making terrific rosés from Sangiovese grapes, which originally come from Tuscany (they're the primary grapes in wines from the Chianti region). Rosés can also be found in Italy, made from either Sangiovese or Nebbiolo grapes.

Cabernet Franc

Made in the Loire region of northern France, Cabernet Franc grapes make a dry, elegant style of rosé. The Chinon and Anjou regions boast particularly elegant pink wines with distinct herbal scents. Lovely rosés of Cabernet Franc can also be found in the New World, particularly in California.

Mourvèdre

Mourvèdre is the primary grape used in the wines of Bandol in northern Provence. In rosé (as well as in red wines), Mourvèdre comprises at least fifty percent of the blend, with Grenache, Syrah, and other grapes lending the balance.

Tempranillo

Tempranillo is often used in the Spanish rosados, particularly in the Rioja region. It is often blended with garnacha, or Grenache, and other local grapes to make pleasing, hearty, rustic wines suitable for everyday drinking.

Sparkling Rosé

Some of the finest examples of sparkling rosé come from Champagne and use the same style of fermentation (see page 36). Some sparkling Champagnes are made using the saignée method (right), while others blend small amounts of still Pinot Noir– or Pinot Meunier–based wine into a white base wine before fermentation. Fine sparkling rosés are also made in Italy, Spain, and California.

The saignée method

The first rosés may have been created by accident, when vintners trying to increase the intensity of their red wine "bled off" some of the pale grape juice from the tank before fermentation. While the remaining grape juice was left in the tank in contact with the grape skins to develop intense color and flavor, the bled juice was fermented separately into a light-bodied, refreshing rosé. Some of the top rosés in France, the U.S., and other winemaking regions are still produced this way using what has become known as the saignée method (saignée means "bled" in French).

Niçoise salad with seared tuna

Pink wines and salads like this are natural partners in the South of France. The wine's acid cuts through the tuna's richness, and balances the assertive olives, anchovies, and vinaigrette.

½ cup plus 1 tsp extra-virgin olive oil, plus more if needed

¼ cup red wine vinegar

1 tbsp Dijon mustard

1 tbsp chopped shallot

1 tbsp fresh tarragon leaves

Kosher salt and freshly ground pepper

½ lb small red or white boiling potatoes

½ lb haricots verts or other small green beans, trimmed

8–12 olive oil–packed anchovy fillets, optional

¼ cup milk, optional

1 piece sashimi-grade tuna fillet, about ¾ lb and 1 inch thick

6–8 cups torn romaine or butter lettuce leaves

4 small tomatoes, chopped

2 hard-boiled eggs, peeled and sliced

½ cup Kalamata olives

In a food processor, combine the ½ cup olive oil, the vinegar, mustard, shallot, tarragon, ½ teaspoon salt, and a few grinds of pepper and process until almost smooth. Taste and adjust the seasonings. Set aside.

In a saucepan, combine the potatoes with salted water to cover, bring to a boil, and cook until tender, about 20 minutes. About 7 minutes before the potatoes are done, add the beans to the water. When the potatoes and beans are tender, drain them and immediately immerse in a large bowl of cold water to halt the cooking. Drain, and then peel the potatoes and cut them into slices ¼ inch thick.

While the vegetables are cooking, in a small bowl, combine the anchovies, if using, and milk and let stand for 10–15 minutes. Drain, discarding the milk. Pat the anchovies dry with paper towels and chop coarsely.

Preheat a cast-iron or other heavy frying pan over high heat until very hot. Add the remaining 1 teaspoon oil and swirl to coat the pan. Add the tuna and cook until seared on the first side, about 2 minutes. Turn the tuna over and sear on the second side, 1–2 minutes. The fish should still be very pink in the center. Transfer the tuna to a cutting board and cut across the grain into slices ¼ inch thick.

In a large bowl, add the lettuce and about 2 tablespoons of the dressing. Toss to coat well and divide among chilled plates. Add the potato slices and beans to the bowl, drizzle with more dressing, and season to taste with salt and pepper. Toss well and divide among the plates. Arrange the anchovies, tomatoes, egg slices, and olives on top of the salads, dividing evenly. Top each serving with one-fourth of the tuna, and drizzle evenly with the remaining dressing. Serve right away.

MAKES 4 SERVINGS

New World match

The tang of a California Vin Gris of Pinot Noir will stand up to the piquant dressing, while its fruitiness will flatter the seared tuna.

Old World match

A sun-kissed Côtes de Provence rosé features olive and herbal aromas and muted fruit flavors that will mingle naturally with the salad's flavors.

Alternative pairings

The effervescence and uncomplicated flavors of a Cava Rosado (Sparkling Wines, page 39) will make a zesty contrast to the multi-layered salad.

A lightly chilled red wine, like a fruity Beaujolais-Villages (Juicy Reds, page 112), will highlight the meatiness of the tuna. The wine's acid will also stand up to the tangy salad dressing.

Coffee-rubbed baby back ribs

Grilling season is always a good time to have rosé on hand. Its fruity character contrasts with the bitter char imparted by the grill and the smoky and spicy flavors found in many spice rubs.

Trim away any surface fat from the ribs. Using a sharp knife, make a vertical slit into the membrane near the center of slab. Lift a corner of the membrane and, using a paper towel to get a good grip, pull it back toward the end of the slab. It should come away in 2 or 3 pieces. Repeat the process on the other side.

In a small bowl, stir together 2 tablespoons of the espresso powder, the brown sugar, chile powder, paprika, cocoa powder, cumin, garlic, 1 teaspoon salt, the cayenne pepper, celery salt, and ½ teaspoon black pepper. Sprinkle the mixture evenly over both sides of each rib rack, and gently massage it into the meat. Wrap the racks in plastic wrap and refrigerate for 1–2 hours. Remove the ribs from the refrigerator about 30 minutes before you plan to start grilling.

Prepare a charcoal or gas grill for indirect-heat cooking over low heat. In a small bowl, stir together the wine, vinegar, remaining 1 teaspoon espresso powder, 1 teaspoon salt, and the pepper sauce to make a glaze.

Place the ribs, bone side down, on the grill rack over the coolest part of the grill. Cover the grill and cook until the meat is very tender and has shrunk away from the ends of the bones, 1¾–2¼ hours total. Every 30 minutes, turn the ribs over and rotate the slabs 180 degrees to ensure even cooking. After 1 hour of cooking, baste the ribs with the glaze and then continue basting every 30 minutes. When the ribs are ready, transfer them to a rimmed baking sheet and sprinkle lightly with salt. Cover with aluminum foil and let rest for 20 minutes.

Using a sharp knife, cut the racks into individual ribs and arrange on a platter. Serve right away.

MAKES 4–6 SERVINGS

New World matches

Sweetly spiced ribs fairly beg for a pink wine, like a Australian rosé of Syrah, with its abundance of sweet fruit and peppery spice.

Try an off-dry California Zinfandel Rosé (as opposed to a typical White Zinfandel). The wine's fruity flavors and hint of sweetness will nicely complement the savory-sweet sauce.

Old World match

The bright acidity of a Navarra or Rioja Rosado will help cut through the ribs' fat while complementing the meat with its ripe fruit.

Alternative pairing

For a southern Italian take, try a Primitivo from Puglia (similar to Zinfandel; Bold Reds, page 143). The wine's aromatic spices and red fruit will flatter the well-spiced meat.

2 racks baby back ribs, each about 2 lb

2 tbsp plus 1 tsp instant espresso powder

1 tbsp firmly packed brown sugar

2 tsp pure chile powder

1 tsp Spanish smoked paprika

1 tsp unsweetened cocoa powder

1 tsp ground cumin

1 tsp granulated garlic

Kosher salt

½ tsp cayenne pepper

½ tsp celery salt

Freshly ground black pepper

⅓ cup dry rosé

2 tbsp balsamic vinegar

¼ tsp hot red pepper sauce such as Tabasco, or to taste

Broiled eggplant with fontina & tomato sauce

The bright, fruity wine offsets the slight bitterness of the eggplant and the richness of the cheese. The wine's lively acidity also cancels out any tartness from the tomato sauce.

1 can (15 oz) tomato sauce

2 tbsp dry white wine or dry vermouth

1 tsp dried basil

1 tsp dried oregano

Freshly ground black pepper

1/2 cup extra-virgin olive oil

1/2 cup fresh basil leaves

3 tbsp fresh lemon juice

2 tsp Dijon mustard

1 clove garlic, finely chopped

Kosher salt

2 large eggplants, about 1¼ lb each, each peeled and cut into 12 slices about 1/2 inch thick

6 oz fontina cheese, coarsely shredded

1/4 cup grated Parmesan cheese

2 tbsp chopped fresh flat-leaf parsley

In a small nonaluminum saucepan, combine the tomato sauce, wine, dried basil, dried oregano, and a few grinds of pepper and bring to a boil over high heat. Reduce the heat to medium and simmer, uncovered, until the sauce thickens slightly and the flavors are blended, about 10 minutes. Remove from the heat and set aside. In a food processor, combine the olive oil, basil, lemon juice, mustard, garlic, and 1/2 teaspoon salt and process until smooth.

Position a rack about 6 inches from the heat source and preheat the broiler. Line 2 rimmed baking sheets with aluminum foil. Brush the eggplant slices on both sides with the oil mixture and arrange them on the prepared baking sheets. Broil 1 sheet until the eggplant is golden brown on the first side, 7–8 minutes, rotating the sheet 180 degrees halfway through. Turn the slices over and broil on the second side, again rotating the sheet at the midpoint, until the eggplant slices are golden brown and tender when pierced with a fork, 6–7 minutes longer. Repeat to broil the second sheet. As each sheet comes out of the broiler, stack the eggplant slices on top of one another and fold the aluminum foil around them, enclosing them completely. Let the slices steam for 4–5 minutes to soften fully.

Preheat the oven to 375°F. Place 8 of the eggplant slices on a baking sheet, spread each slice with 1–2 teaspoons of the tomato sauce, and sprinkle with a thin layer of the fontina. Repeat the layers—eggplant slice, sauce, fontina—twice. Sprinkle the Parmesan evenly over the top.

Bake the stacks until the cheese is melted and the layers are heated through, 10–12 minutes. Divide among warmed individual plates and garnish with the parsley. Serve right away.

MAKES 4 MAIN-COURSE SERVINGS, OR 8 FIRST-COURSE SERVINGS

New World match

The natural acidity of a California Rosé of Sangiovese will help take the edge off the sauce's tang as it cuts through the richness of the melted cheese.

Old World match

For a more traditional connection to the dish, try a Tuscan Sangiovese Rosato. The wine's herbal notes and cherry tomato nuances will echo similar flavors in the dish.

Alternative pairings

A mouthwatering, but lightly tannic Barbera d'Alba (Juicy Reds, page 113) would also work well here. Its mild astringence will mute the eggplant's bitterness.

Choose a Garnacha from Catalonia (Juicy Reds, page 113), whose red fruit flavors will highlight the hint of sweetness in the concentrated sauce.

Chicken & sausage paella

The fruit-forward wine contrasts nicely to the rich chicken meat and smoky chorizo in this traditional Spanish dish. Light in body, the wine forms a textural counterpoint to the granular rice.

6–7 cups reduced-sodium chicken broth

1/4 tsp saffron threads

8–10 skinless, boneless chicken thighs, about 2 lb total weight

1 slice pancetta, about 3 oz and 1/4 inch thick

1/2 lb fully cooked Spanish chorizo sausage

1/3 cup extra-virgin olive oil

1/2 tsp red pepper flakes, or to taste

1 yellow onion, minced

2 tomatoes, peeled, seeded, and chopped

4 cloves garlic, minced

1 tsp mild smoked Spanish paprika

3 cups Spanish Bomba rice

2 tsp kosher salt

1 cup diced roasted red bell pepper

1 cup shelled and peeled fava beans or shelled English peas

1/4 cup minced fresh flat-leaf parsley

Preheat the oven to 400°F. In a saucepan over low heat, combine the chicken broth and saffron and bring just to a simmer. Cut the chicken thighs into bite-sized pieces, then cut the pancetta into 1/2-inch dice. Finally, cut the sausage into thin slices.

In a 17- to 18-inch paella pan or other ovenproof shallow pan, warm the oil over high heat. Add the chicken pieces and sauté, turning frequently, until lightly browned on both sides but not fully cooked, 4–5 minutes. Using a slotted spoon, transfer the chicken to a platter. Reduce the heat to medium-low and add the pancetta, chorizo, and red pepper flakes. Cook, stirring occasionally, until the meats render some of their fat, 1–2 minutes.

Add the onion to the pan and sauté until the onion is soft and translucent, 3–4 minutes. Add the tomatoes, garlic, and paprika and cook, stirring, until fragrant, about 2 minutes. Add the rice and stir to coat evenly with the seasonings. Add 6 cups of the hot broth, the chicken pieces, and the salt. Raise the heat to medium-high and bring to a boil. Adjust the heat as needed to maintain a slow boil and cook for about 5 minutes. Gently stir in the roasted pepper and fava beans and transfer the pan to the oven. Bake, uncovered, until the rice is almost al dente, 12–15 minutes. (After baking, if there is still liquid in the pan, return the pan to the stove top over high heat and cook undisturbed until the liquid evaporates. If the paella is dry but the rice is not yet nearly tender, drizzle with 1/4 cup hot broth and bake for 2–3 minutes longer.)

Remove from the oven, taste, and adjust the seasonings. Cover the pan with aluminum foil and let stand until the rice is tender, 5–10 minutes. Uncover, garnish with the parsley, and serve directly from the pan.

MAKES 8–10 SERVINGS

New World match

A plummy Argentine Malbec Rosé will contrast nicely with the spicy, salty, smoky, and meaty flavors of the dish.

Old World match

A rosé from France's Languedoc region— a blend of Grenache, Syrah and Carignan— will highlight both the saffron and red pepper in the paella.

Alternative pairings

Choose an unoaked Rioja sin Crianza (Smooth Reds, page 127) whose soft tannins will stand up to the rich chicken and smoky sausage.

For a match that literally bubbles with contrasts, try a California Blanc de Noirs (Sparkling Wines, page 39). The wine's effervescence will recharge the palate between bites.

Halibut with spring vegetable ragout

A light-bodied wine forms a textural contrast to the meaty fish. For best results, choose a bone-dry rosé, which will take on a pleasantly sweet taste from the reaction with the artichokes.

2 Yukon gold potatoes, about 10 oz total weight

1 package frozen artichoke hearts, thawed

1 leek, white part only, cut into slices 1/2 inch thick

3 cloves garlic, thinly sliced

1 3/4 cups reduced-sodium chicken broth

1 tsp fresh thyme leaves

1 bay leaf

Kosher salt and freshly ground black pepper

Pinch of red pepper flakes

2 slices thick-cut bacon, cut into 1/2 inch pieces

1/2 lb mixed mushrooms, brushed clean, tough stems removed, and cut into 1/2 inch pieces

1 tbsp sherry vinegar

1 tbsp extra-virgin olive oil

1 1/2 lb skinless halibut fillets

2 tbsp minced fresh flat-leaf parsley

Peel the potatoes and cut them into 3/4-inch cubes. In a large saucepan, combine the potatoes, artichokes, leek, garlic, broth, thyme, bay leaf, 1/2 teaspoon salt, a few grinds of black pepper, and the red pepper flakes and bring to a boil over medium-high heat. Reduce the heat to low, cover, and simmer until the vegetables are tender, 10–12 minutes.

While the vegetables are cooking, in a frying pan over medium heat, cook the bacon until crisp, stirring occasionally, 3–4 minutes. Transfer to paper towels to drain. With the pan still over medium heat, add the mushrooms to the bacon fat and season with salt and pepper. Sauté the mushrooms until tender and lightly browned, 3–4 minutes. Add the vinegar and cook for 1 minute. Remove from the heat.

When the vegetables are ready, remove from the heat and remove and discard the bay leaf. Stir in the mushrooms and cover to keep warm.

Heat a large nonstick frying pan over medium-high heat for 2–3 minutes, until hot. Add the oil and swirl to coat the pan. Add the halibut and sauté, turning once, until nicely browned on both sides and opaque throughout when tested with a knife tip, about 8 minutes total. Transfer the halibut to a cutting board. Cut the fillets into large, equal pieces.

Divide the vegetable mixture among warmed shallow soup bowls. Top each bowl with the halibut pieces, dividing evenly, and garnish with the reserved bacon and the parsley. Serve right away.

MAKES 4 SERVINGS

New World match

An austere cranberry-scented Pinot Noir Rosé from Oregon will contrast nicely with both the mild fish and the vegetables in the ragout.

Old World match

Choose a light Loire Chinon or Bourgueil rosé, made from Cabernet Franc, whose hint of earthiness will reference the mushrooms.

Alternative pairings

A Sauvignon Blanc from New Zealand (Crisp Whites, page 52) will taste fruitier, thanks to the artichokes, and a bit softer and rounder, providing a pleasing textural complement.

For another example of the way artichokes can influence a pairing, try a lemony Greek Moschofilero (similar to Grüner Veltliner; Soft Whites, page 69). The artichoke will help to open the wine's delicate flavors.

Juicy reds

Ripe, luscious, and accessible, juicy reds are packed with bright fruit flavors. They are the perfect warm-weather party wines, matching an array of different dishes and tastes.

Versatile and easy to drink, juicy reds are imbued with ripe, fruity flavors. They are the "table wines" in villages across France and Italy, served in carafes and paired with the local cuisine. French Beaujolais, made from the Gamay grape, is the quintessential example of a juicy red, but similar light-bodied, fruit-forward wines are popular choices in many wine-growing regions, more often in the Old World than the New. Uncomplicated, low in alcohol, and meant to be consumed young, juicy reds go well with a variety of casual dishes, from picnic fare to light pasta dishes to rustic stews. Some fans of juicy red wines serve the wines lightly chilled to enhance their refreshing qualities.

About juicy reds

Well known for their easy drinking qualities, juicy reds are the drink of choice for those who desire a refreshing, tannin-free red wine. These wines are high in acid, food friendly, and created to be drunk young. Most juicy reds are not aged in oak, which preserves their distinct fruit flavors. This, and the fact that these wines are typically relatively low in alcohol, keeps them straightforward and approachable.

Wine temperature

Sweet and sparkling wines are both delicious served very cold. Other whites show best when slightly warmer. Conversely, and contrary to popular belief, many red wines benefit from being slightly colder than the customary room temperature. For the best flavor, remove crisp or soft whites from the refrigerator 15 minutes or so before you plan to serve them, and a little longer for rich whites. If a smooth or bold red wine seems too warm, put it in the refrigerator for 15–30 minutes. A juicy red wine can be chilled for up to 1 hour.

Attributes of juicy reds

Aging in oak adds complexity to a wine and bumps up the price. Juicy reds see little, if any, oak, so their fruit flavors remain prominent, and the wines remain relatively simple and tend to be inexpensive. These wines are a popular choice for new wine drinkers who are just beginning to explore red wines.

Like pink wines (see page 95), juicy reds can bridge the gap when you are serving foods that can be paired with either a white or a red wine, although they don't match well with subtle, complex dishes, which can overwhelm the wine's simple nature. But these decidedly unserious but nevertheless appealing wines are a good match for informal dishes. In the Old World, where wine drinking is a daily occurrence, juicy reds are paired with everyday meals. In the New World, juicy reds are offered with casual foods—think pizza, burgers, and simple pasta dishes—with great success. They are the perfect wines to complement foods coated in barbecue sauce: the wine's acidity stands up the sauce's tanginess. At the same time, the sauce's slight sweetness complements the wine's fruitiness. In addition, the smoky flavor imparted from cooking over a charcoal grill nicely plays off the fruit flavors in the wine. The refreshing qualities of juicy reds are enhanced when they are lightly chilled (see left), which makes them the perfect red wine style for summertime dining.

1 **Look**
Since juicy reds are meant to be consumed soon after bottling, expect them to be bright in color and to range in hue from purple-blue to cherry-red. Whatever color the wine, it should appear vivid, which is a good indication that the wine is still young (wines tend to turn browner as they age).

2 **Swirl**
As the wine moves around the glass, it will appear on the thin side for a red wine, hinting at its light body and low alcohol content. Any legs will dissipate quickly.

3 **Smell**
No matter what the varietal, the wine should smell fresh, bright, and fruity. Some use the term "grapey" to describe the aroma of juicy reds, which refers both to their straightforward aromas and the fact that the flavors of these uncomplicated wines can seem to some closer to grape juice than fine wine.

4 **Sip**
Juicy reds will not express much complexity on the palate, but this is not necessarily a bad thing. Wines of this style are made to be uncomplicated and accessible, as is the food they are typically paired with. Expect a light body and short finish, which may explain why some aficionados describe juicy reds as "gulpable."

Flavor profile

Juicy red wines are very popular in the Old World. Nearly every village in winemaking regions produces a simple local table wine, which pairs effortlessly with the local cuisine. Wine drinkers in the New World typically favor more showy, deeply extracted wines, but the juicy style of reds is enjoying increased popularity in recent years, particularly among people who have traveled widely abroad.

Cherry

The bright aroma and flavor of fresh cherries is prominent throughout the juicy red category.

Dried Cherry

Wines from hot climates often take on the concentrated flavor of dried cherries.

Raspberry

The smell of fresh raspberries comes through in nearly every wine in the juicy red category.

Plum

Plummy, jammy flavors characterize many of the juicy reds from Italy and beyond.

Strawberry

If you smell or taste fresh, ripe strawberries, even strawberry jam, in a red wine, odds are that it's from the juicy category.

Lavender

Juicy reds from the south of France often feature lavender scents, which could come from the native herbs prolific in the region.

Banana

It may sound strange, but close your eyes and taste a Beaujolais and you may detect the distinctive flavor of banana along with the red fruits.

Pomegranate

Tart and slightly astringent, the flavor perception of pomegranate is common in slightly tannic juicy reds such as Dolcetto.

Herbs

Herbal scents help round out the red fruit flavors in the juicy reds, giving them increased dimension and interest.

Minerals

The mineral-rich soil of many Old World vineyards contributes its flavor to a variety of juicy reds.

Key juicy red wines

When buying a juicy red, look for the most recent vintage and drink it right away, as it will show its best qualities when young; juicy wines left to age can become dull, flavorless, and harshly acidic. A juicy red should also be low in alcohol, which contributes to the wine's refreshing nature. Keep a supply of juicy reds on hand in the summer months to serve with the season's casual cuisine.

Négociants

Common in Burgundy, *négociants* are middle-men, or merchants, who buy grapes, grape juice, or leftover finished wine from growers or producers. *Négociants* may crush, ferment, and age the grapes, or simply bottle the wine before distributing it to the marketplace. Some stalwarts believe a *négociant*-produced wine is of lesser quality than that made by a long-standing chateau, but the truth is that there are many good *négociants* who value quality as much as an independent wine house.

Gamay

Gamay, with its appealing red-berry fruit, is the primary grape in the wines of Beaujolais on the southern end of Burgundy in France. There, Gamay forms the basis for two basic wine styles, Beaujolias Nouveau and Cru Beaujolais. Beaujolais Nouveau is released on the third Thursday of November following the year's harvest. The word "nouveau" refers to the fact that the wine is very young, or new. Much hyped, the wine is rushed to Paris's cafés still in the barrel. Some of the excitement has carried over to the U.S., where it's common to find Beaujolais Nouveau at French restaurants during the late autumn and early winter. It is also a popular companion to the Thanksgiving meal, as the wine is released shortly before the holiday and its straightforward flavors match well to a wide range of the traditional foods. Cru Beaujolais is a deeper and more complex version of the wine, yet still simple, fruit forward, and best when drunk young.

All types of Beaujolais are great values when compared to many other types of red wine. A California grape that many people thought was Gamay and that shared its straightforward characteristics, has now been identified as a different grape called Valdigué.

Pinot Noir

Pinot Noir has a dual personality, fitting equally well into the juicy reds and smooth reds categories. Burgundy sets the standard for fine Pinot Noir–based wines; there, the varietal is the only grape allowed by law to be included in red wines. If you are looking for a Pinot Noir in a juicy style, with little or no oak influence, look for an inexpensive bottle (smooth-style Pinot Noirs can be pricey) from a recent vintage. It may say Bourgogne Rouge on the label or feature the name of a village, both of which indicate that the wine is simple and straightforward. (Wines with the words "Grand Cru" or "Premier Cru" are usually better suited to the smooth red category; see page 126.) In Burgundy, this style of wine is the perfect partner for some of the region's classic rustic dishes, such as *coq au vin* and *boeuf Bourguignon*. The French regions of Alsace and the Loire also produce intriguing versions of Pinot Noir–based wines with a more minerally profile than that of Burgundy. New Zealand also produces fine Pinot Noirs in a juicy style.

Cabernet Franc

Widely used as a blending grape in Bordeaux wines, Cabernet Franc shines on its own in cool climates, such as France's Loire Valley. There it makes lovely, light-bodied, and fruit-forward wines, the best-known being Chinon, which is at its juicy best when young. Cabernet Franc also forms delicious light reds in the Friuli region of northeast Italy and in northern California and Washington State. Cabernet Franc is a great wine choice for fans of Cabernet Sauvignon who are looking for a lighter, less harsh wine to match with a meal, as the two have similar flavor profiles. Cabernet Franc's herbal-vegetal character makes it a good match for vegetables, which can be tricky to pair with other red wines.

Valpolicella

Corvina, along with Rondinella and Molinara grapes, make this standout juicy red from the Veneto in Italy. Like all juicy reds, Valpolicella is simple and straightforward, meant for everyday drinking. For the best quality, look for a Valpolicella "Classico." When seeking out a juicy red, avoid Valpolicella labeled "Amarone," which is a bold red wine, or "Recioto," which is a sweet wine.

Dolcetto

This Italian grape is grown chiefly in the Piedmont region of northern Italy. Its name implies sweetness ("dolcetto" means "little sweet one" in Italian), but in fact the wine is very dry. Dolcetto's high acid marries well with tomatoes, which can be tricky to match to wine, as the two acids cancel each other out. Some Dolcettos may be a bit more tannic than other wines in this category; ask a trusted wine merchant to guide you when choosing.

Barbera

Another wine native to Piedmont, Italy, is Barbera. This straightforward red wine can be found in households and cafés throughout the region. Look to wines labeled "Barbera d'Alba" or "Barbera d'Asti" to be of high quality and consistency. In the New World, Barbera is now being produced in California.

Grenache

Known more for its role in Rhone-style blends, such as in Côtes-du-Rhône rouge, Grenache also makes a simple grapey wine on its own in warm Mediterranean regions and in Australia.

Red wine and fish

Traditional thinking warns us that red wine paired with fish is a recipe for disaster. But cooks in Oregon use the following strategies to pair the two seemingly incompatible ingredients successfully: First, they begin with an impeccably fresh product that is not too "fishy," such as locally caught wild salmon. Next, they choose a wine that is low in tannin and high in acid, as is a juicy Pinot Noir. Finally, they employ a cooking method—such as pan searing—and add companion ingredients—such as foraged wild mushrooms—to reinforce the link to the wine.

Savory cheesecake

The best red wines to serve with appetizers are light, fruity, and high in acid. Here these qualities combine to cut the richness of the cheeses and stand up to the tangy roasted peppers.

1 head garlic

1 tablespoon extra-virgin olive oil

$1/2$ cup fine dried bread crumbs

3 tbsp grated Parmesan cheese

$1/2$ tsp sweet paprika

Kosher salt

2 tbsp unsalted butter, melted

$3/4$ lb cream cheese, at room temperature

$1/4$ lb blue cheese such as Roquefort or Maytag Blue, at room temperature

2 eggs

1 tbsp finely chopped fresh tarragon

$1/2$ tsp dry mustard

$1/2$ tsp celery salt

Freshly ground pepper

$1/3$ cup diced roasted red bell pepper

Preheat the oven to 425°F. Cut the top $1/2$ inch from the garlic head, place the head in a small baking dish, drizzle with the oil, and cover with aluminum foil. Bake until the garlic is soft, about 45 minutes. When cool, squeeze the garlic pulp out of the skins. Set aside 2 tablespoons roasted garlic pulp and reserve the rest for another use.

Reduce the oven heat to 300°F. Spray an 8-inch springform pan with nonstick cooking spray. In a small bowl, stir together the bread crumbs, Parmesan, paprika, and $1/4$ teaspoon salt. Stir in the melted butter, mixing until the dry ingredients are evenly moistened. Pour the mixture evenly over the bottom of the prepared pan and pat it firmly in place with the bottom of a small glass. Bake until the crust is firm and lightly browned, 6–8 minutes. Let cool on a rack for 10–15 minutes.

With a mixer on medium speed, beat the cream cheese and blue cheese until smooth. Add the eggs one at a time, beating each until well blended. Add the garlic pulp, the tarragon, mustard, celery salt, and a few grinds of pepper and mix well. Fold in the roasted pepper with a rubber spatula.

Pour the filling evenly over the crust. Bake the cheesecake until the filling is puffed and lightly browned, about 1 hour and 20 minutes. Transfer the pan to a rack and let cool for 15 minutes. Run a sharp knife blade around the edge of the cheesecake to loosen it from the pan sides, then release and remove the pan sides. Let the cheesecake cool to room temperature.

Slide the cheesecake onto a platter. Cut the cheesecake into thin wedges and serve at room temperature.

MAKES 8–10 SERVINGS

New World match

Look for a light-bodied Pinot Noir from New Zealand, whose bright acidity will elevate the rich cheesecake.

Old World match

A Cru Beaujolais from the villages of Fleurie or Morgon forms a fruity contrast to the rich, salty cheese.

Alternative pairings

A luscious Chardonnay from California's Sonoma Valley (Rich Whites, page 82) matches the dish's creamy texture.

A fruity, dry sparkling rosé from France's Loire Valley (Sparkling Wines, page 39) is a nice foil for the bold flavors.

Capellini with tomatoes, basil & fresh mozzarella

This simple pasta dish is balanced by a wine with high acid to match that of the tomatoes, while contrasting with the creamy cheese. Fresh basil is echoed in a wine with an herbal aroma.

3 large, ripe tomatoes, about 1½ lb total weight, peeled, seeded, and coarsely chopped

3 cloves garlic, minced

2 tbsp extra-virgin olive oil

2 tbsp chopped fresh basil

2 tbsp chopped fresh flat-leaf parsley

1 tbsp minced fresh chives

Kosher salt

½ tsp freshly ground black pepper

¾ lb dried capellini

½ cup finely diced fresh mozzarella or fontina cheese

½ cup freshly grated Parmesan cheese

In a frying pan large enough to hold the cooked pasta and sauce, combine the tomatoes, garlic, oil, basil, parsley, chives, 1 teaspoon salt, and pepper. Let stand at room temperature while you cook the pasta.

Bring a large pot three-fourths full of salted water to a boil. Add the capellini and cook until al dente, 3–4 minutes or according to the package directions. Just before the pasta is ready, place the frying pan with the tomato mixture over medium heat and gently bring the sauce just to a simmer. When the pasta is ready, drain it well, then add it to the pan with the simmering sauce. Add the mozzarella and toss to combine.

Divide the pasta among warmed shallow bowls and serve right away. Pass the Parmesan cheese at the table.

MAKES 4 SERVINGS

New World match

Australian Grenache provides both ripe red fruit and mouthwatering acidity to complement the tomatoes in this dish.

Old World match

A cherry-spiked Dolcetto from northern Italy will echo the tomatoes' sweetness.

Alternative pairings

Highlight the dish's subtle herb flavors with a grassy, lemon-laced Sauvignon Blanc from New Zealand (Crisp Whites, page 52).

A Sangiovese rosé (Pink Wines, page 99) will match the acid of the tomatoes and cut through the rich cheese.

Italian-style vegetable & bread soup

Meaty pancetta and chewy cannellini beans form a bridge to the wine, whose acid mirrors that of the tomatoes. Day-old bread lends texture to the soup to contrast with the wine's light body.

Cut the pancetta into 1-inch pieces. In a large, heavy saucepan over low heat, warm the oil. Add the pancetta and sauté until it starts to crisp, 3–4 minutes. Add the onion, carrot, celery, garlic, and pepper flakes and cook, stirring occasionally, until the vegetables are soft, about 10 minutes. Add the tomatoes with their juice, the broth, parsley, 1 teaspoon salt, and a few grindings of black pepper. Raise the heat to medium-high and bring to a boil. Reduce the heat to low and simmer, uncovered, for 10 minutes.

Drain 1 can of the beans, reserving the liquid. Place the beans in a small bowl and mash roughly with a fork. Add the mashed beans and the whole beans with the liquid from both cans to the simmering vegetables and cook for 5 minutes. Add the zucchini and yellow squash, green and red cabbage, and Swiss chard and continue to cook until the cabbage is tender, 10–15 minutes longer.

Stir in the bread cubes and continue to cook over medium-low heat until the bread has absorbed most of the liquid, about 10 minutes. Taste and adjust the seasonings.

Ladle the soup into warmed shallow bowls and serve right away.

MAKES 4–6 SERVINGS

3 oz sliced pancetta

2 tbsp extra-virgin olive oil

1 yellow onion, minced

1 large carrot, minced

1 celery stalk, minced

4 cloves garlic, chopped

1/4 tsp red pepper flakes

1 can (14 oz) diced tomatoes

1 3/4 cups reduced-sodium chicken broth

1/4 cup chopped fresh flat-leaf parsley

Kosher salt and freshly ground black pepper

2 cans (15 oz) cannellini beans

1 *each* zucchini and yellow squash, halved lengthwise, and thinly sliced

4 cups thinly sliced mixed green and red cabbage

2 cups coarsely chopped Swiss chard leaves

4 cups cubed day-old coarse country bread (1-inch cubes)

New World match

The unique blend of earthiness and fruitiness in a California Cabernet Franc will echo the soup's bean and tomato base.

Old World match

A young, fruity Spanish Garnacha from Jumilla has just the right heft to match the soup's slow-cooked flavors.

Alternative pairings

To flatter the vegetables, try a full-flavored Fumé Blanc from northern California (Rich Whites, page 83).

A Côtes-du-Ventoux from the southern Rhône (Smooth Reds, page 127) pairs fruity Grenache with spicy Syrah to enhance the soup.

Grilled sausages with lentil salad

A light, fruity wine forms a pleasing contrast with the dense texture and meaty flavor of the sausages and the hint of chile. Earthy lentils can reflect similar qualities in the wine.

1 cup green lentils

2 whole cloves

1 yellow onion, halved through the stem end, plus ½ cup finely chopped onion

1 bay leaf

3 carrots, peeled and cut into ⅛-inch dice (about 1 cup)

Kosher salt

3 tbsp extra-virgin olive oil

2 cloves garlic, finely chopped

¼ tsp red pepper flakes

2 tbsp sherry or balsamic vinegar

½ tsp Dijon mustard

Freshly ground black pepper

6 sweet Italian fennel sausages, about ¼ lb each

¼ cup chopped fresh flat-leaf parsley

To make the salad, pick over the lentils, discarding any misshapen ones or tiny stones, then rinse and drain. Fill a saucepan three-fourths full of water and bring to a boil over high heat. Stick a clove in each onion half and add the onion halves to the boiling water with the lentils and bay leaf. Reduce the heat to low, cover, and simmer until the lentils are tender to the bite, 20–25 minutes. Start checking the lentils after about 15 minutes so they don't become mushy.

Remove the lentils from the heat and drain through a sieve, discarding the liquid. Discard the onion halves and bay leaf and transfer the lentils to a serving bowl. Cook the carrots in boiling salted water over high heat until tender-crisp, 2–3 minutes. Drain the carrots and add to the lentils.

In a frying pan over medium-low heat, warm 1 tablespoon of the oil. Add the chopped onion to the pan and sauté until soft and translucent, 3–4 minutes. Add the garlic and pepper flakes and cook, stirring, until fragrant, about 1 minute. Add the onion mixture to the lentils and carrots.

In a small bowl, whisk together the remaining 2 tablespoons olive oil, the vinegar, mustard, ½ teaspoon salt, and a few grinds of pepper. Pour over the warm lentil mixture and toss gently to combine.

Prepare a charcoal or gas grill for direct-heat cooking over medium heat. Place the sausages on the grill rack and cook, turning as needed to brown and cook evenly, until golden brown on all sides and cooked through when tested with a knife tip, 6–8 minutes.

Arrange the sausages on warmed individual plates and spoon the lentil salad alongside. Garnish with the parsley and serve right away.

MAKES 4–6 SERVINGS

New World match

To enhance the flavor of the lentils, as well as the grilled sausages, select a smoky Cabernet Franc from Washington State.

Old World match

Valpolicella's earthy components flatter any dish featuring legumes.

Alternative pairings

A robust Syrah Rosé (Pink Wines, page 98) is a fruit-driven partner to this rustic dish.

A fruity Malbec from the Mendoza region in Argentina (Smooth Reds, page 127) will stand up to the sausage.

Braised beef with herbes de Provence

This meaty stew forms a rustic match with a light, simple wine, reminiscent of the table wines of southern France. Fragrant herbs and tart tomatoes match similar flavors in the wine.

2 tbsp extra-virgin olive oil

4 slices thick-cut bacon, cut into 1-inch pieces

5 tbsp all-purpose flour

Kosher salt and freshly ground black pepper

4–5 lb meaty beef shanks, about 1½ inches thick

1 *each* yellow onion and large carrot, coarsely chopped

4 cloves garlic, crushed

1 can (14½ oz) reduced-sodium beef broth

3 cups juicy red wine

1 tbsp tomato paste

2 thin strips orange zest

1 tsp herbes de Provence

1 tbsp soft unsalted butter

⅓ cup *each* chopped oil-packed sun-dried tomatoes and coarsely chopped Kalamata olives

Hot cooked buttered egg noodles for serving

3 tbsp chopped fresh flat-leaf parsley

Preheat the oven to 300°F. In a Dutch oven, warm the oil over medium heat. Add the bacon and sauté until it renders its fat but is not crisp, about 3–4 minutes. Using a slotted spoon, transfer the bacon to a plate. Stir together 4 tablespoons of the flour, 1 teaspoon salt, and a few grinds of pepper. Lightly dust the beef shanks with the seasoned flour. Return the pot to medium-high heat. Working in batches, brown the shanks in the fat on all sides, about 5–7 minutes total for each batch. Transfer the shanks to a platter. Add the onion, carrot, and garlic and stir to scrape up the browned bits on the pan bottom. Add the broth, wine, tomato paste, and orange zest and bring to a boil. Stir in the herbes de Provence, 1½ teaspoons salt, and a few grinds of pepper. Return the shanks to the pot, cover, and place in the oven. Braise until the meat is very tender, about 2 hours. Turn the shanks over after 1 hour of cooking.

Transfer the meat and garlic cloves to a platter. Pour the contents of the pot through a medium-mesh sieve into a bowl. Using the back of a spoon, press firmly against the vegetables to extract as much liquid as possible. Discard the contents of the sieve. Using a large spoon, skim off and discard the surface fat and return the liquid to the pot.

In a small bowl, mix the remaining 1 tablespoon flour and the butter to make a paste. Return the pot to medium heat and bring to a boil. Whisk in the paste a little at a time, until the sauce just begins to thicken. Adjust the seasonings, then remove from the heat. Discard the bones and tough skin from the shanks, reserving the meat. Pull the meat into large chunks, and add the meat, tomatoes, and olives to the pot. Simmer over low heat for 15–20 minutes to blend the flavors. Divide the noodles among warmed shallow bowls, and arrange some of the meat on top. Spoon the sauce over the meat and the noodles, sprinkle with parsley, and serve.

MAKES 6 SERVINGS

New World match

A Rhône-style blend from the Central Coast of California will offer a fruity contrast to the stew's meatiness.

Old World match

Choose a ripe, rustic, Côtes-de-Provence red to echo the stew's herbal flavors and cut through its richness.

Alternative pairings

For an interesting white pairing, try a fragrant, Viognier-based Condrieu from the northern Rhône (Rich Whites, page 82).

Choose a hearty Tuscan Brunello de Montalcino (Bold Reds, page 143) to echo the stew's slow-cooked flavors.

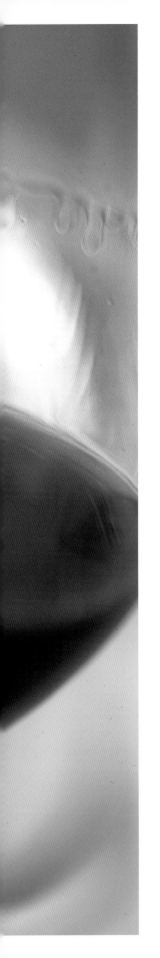

Smooth reds

Spicy, earthy, and supple, smooth reds offer a pleasing blend of soft-textured fruit flavors. Nicely balanced, they often feature smoky, herbal, or vanilla essences to enhance the fruit.

Smooth reds have a smart balance of acidity, earthiness, silkiness, and red fruit flavors. Merlot, which has captured the U.S. wine market by storm, is a prime example of a smooth red, but it is by no means the only wine in this category. Wine-producing regions throughout the world have built grand traditions on these well-crafted, early-drinking reds that can boast herbs, sweet spices, and lots of berry flavors. Smooth reds are versatile, matching with a variety of dishes, from rich poultry to red meats. Almost universally appealing, smooth reds are a sensible choice to offer at a dinner party, especially when hosting a group of people with potentially different preferences.

About smooth reds

Like many red wines, smooth reds feature aromas of berry-cherry fruits, with earthy, herbal, or spicy overtones. But what sets them apart from other red styles is that their taste elements—acidity, sweetness, and bitterness—are all in balance. In addition, smooth reds are noticeably soft in texture. Smooth reds are typically medium in body with a velvety mouthfeel, giving them universal appeal.

Wine legs

This tasting term for the tracks left on the inside of the glass when a wine is swirled, also called tears, has sparked much debate. At one time, pronounced legs in wine were thought be a sign of quality, but this is not necessarily the case. In truth, the appearance of fat, slow-moving tears only indicates that the wine is full in body and high in alcohol—possibly sweet—but little else. There are many poor-quality wines on the market with distinct legs, just as there are many high-quality, light-bodied wines that show nearly imperceptible ones.

Attributes of smooth reds

Since smooth reds have more pronounced tannins—albeit soft ones—than the previous wine styles, their qualities are best shown when paired with food. Smooth wines are versatile food companions, matching equally well with roast chicken or pan-fried beef medallions. That said, since they are so subtle, it's best not to pair smooth reds with rich, fatty meats or bold spices, both of which could overwhelm this style of wine. For the best match, choose dishes that are medium in weight, with well-integrated flavors. Simple roasts or straightforward braises are traditional companions.

Precisely because smooth reds are so versatile, it is difficult to pinpoint specific foods that pair well with them. But there are a number of things you can do to ensure a good wine match. For example, to reinforce the link to a smooth red wine, try to employ a cooking method—sautéing, roasting, or braising—that uses browning in the preparation. If the wine has an herbal component, add a handful of fresh herbs to the dish to help it better match to the wine. If you detect an earthy aroma in the wine, consider using mushrooms in the recipe. A wine with pronounced oak flavors can be paired successfully with grilled foods. Finally, smooth reds that show exuberant fruit flavors can stand up well to sauces or stuffings based on similar types of fruit.

1 Look

Smooth reds range in color from bright or deep ruby red to brick red. Regardless of the hue, the wine should appear clear.

2 Swirl

Smooth reds can be relatively high in alcohol, causing the liquid to seem slightly thick as you swirl it and hinting at the wine's medium body. You may see distinct legs on the side of the glass, which further confirms the alcohol present in the wine.

3 Smell

Smooth wines typically smell first of fruit. Some are underscored by intriguing vanilla or smoke nuances, which indicate they were aged in oak. You might also detect the smell of freshly turned earth, mushrooms, or truffles, which reflect each wine's *terroir*. Vegetal or herbal flavors are also common.

4 Sip

Smooth reds are nicely balanced with fruity, oaky, and acidic flavors all in harmony. The fruit will be succulent, ranging from ripe cherries to dark blackberries. The tannins will be soft and round, contributing to the overall smooth impression. Medium in body, the wines leave a feeling in the mouth that is something like two-percent milk. The finish will be medium to long, depending on the varietal's strength and the wine's complexity.

Flavor profile

Smooth reds from the Old World tend to be complex and refined, with a strong sense of place. Grown and made on the same land for centuries, these wines are often blended to achieve the desired balance of flavors and textures. Smooth reds from the New World tend to have more vivacious fruit flavors. Nevertheless, the wines will still be elegant, soft, and accessible.

Dried cherry

The concentrated flavor of dried cherries is typical in wines from warmer climates; cooler climate wines feature fresh cherry scents.

Plum

Dark red fruits such as plum are commonly associated with smooth reds, especially Merlot.

Blackberry

Merlot, Pinot Noir, Barbera, and many other smooth red wines have pronounced dark berry fruit aromas and flavors.

Star anise

Some smooth reds form a subcategory of spicy reds, referring to their scents and flavors of spices (not chiles).

Cinnamon

Sweet spices, such as those you would use to bake cookies, are often perceived in smooth red wines.

Raspberry

Cooler climates produce wines with brighter red fruits, such as fresh raspberries.

Chocolate

A chocolatey aroma or flavor in a smooth red comes from the oak aging. It should be nicely balanced to complement the fruit.

Green bell pepper

The sent of green bell peppers is a telltale sign that a smooth red wine is Merlot or has some in its blend.

Lavender

A floral and herbal scent, such as you find in wild lavender, is often attributed to smooth reds.

Black pepper

Light peppery scents go hand-in-hand with the fruit aromas in an array of smooth reds.

Key smooth red wines

Look for smooth reds that are on the young side, though some can take a small amount of aging. The price of the wine can be a clue—inexpensive wines are typically made to be consumed young, while more expensive wines often need a bit of aging to smooth any rough edges. For the best examples of smooth reds, look for an alcohol content that does not exceed 13 percent.

Quality in Burgundy

In Burgundy, France, the vineyard is considered the most important element in winemaking. Each wine is labeled to indicate its relative quality based on its individual *terroir*. The best vineyards are labeled "Grands Crus" ("cru" means growth), followed closely by "Premiers Crus." Next come village-level wines, which will list a specific village on the label, such as Meursault or Gevrey-Chambertin. The last category includes regional wines, such as Bourgogne Blanc or Bourgogne Rouge, which can be made anywhere in the Burgundy region.

Merlot

Long an important grape in Bordeaux, France, Merlot was once thought of elsewhere only as blending grape used to soften Cabernet Sauvignon–based wines. It has now come into its own in both the Old and New Worlds, rivaled in popularity only by Chardonnay. The original examples of single-varietal Merlot come from the Pomerol and St-Emilion regions in Bordeaux, where it makes a silky wine with lush cherry and blackberry fruit with traces of spice and earth. Based on Merlot's tremendous popularity, other Old World regions are now planting the non-native Merlot grapes, including northern Italy and southwestern France. The New World makes Merlot with intense, concentrated fruit flavors layered with sweet spices and dark chocolate. Some of the best examples come from Napa Valley in California, Washington State, Chile, and Australia. Because of its soft tannins and velvety mouthfeel, Merlot is a great wine for those who like Cabernet Sauvignon's similar flavor profile but are not fans of Cabernet's harsher flavors and texture. Extremely accessible, Merlot is ready to drink almost as soon as it is bottled, whereas Cabernet Sauvignon needs a little age to be palatable.

Pinot Noir

Pinot Noir can be expressed in two main ways: in a juicy red style (see page 112), usually found in the Old World, and in a smooth red style, often made in the New World. In the United States, very good Pinot Noirs are made in California and Oregon, where they grow best in the cooler parts of the states. In California, Sonoma, Napa, and Santa Barbara are prime locations for Pinot Noir; in Oregon, the Willamette Valley boasts perfect growing conditions. Smooth-style Pinot Noirs—with their forward fruit aromas, subtle oak flavors, and soft tannins—are fantastic food wines, handling a variety of foods, even moderately spicy dishes, with ease. For this reason, Pinot Noirs are often recommended by restaurant sommeliers to large groups of diners as wines to match a variety of dishes. In the Old World, look for smooth-style Pinot Noirs from the better-known producers of Burgundy, and in those to which a village or vineyard name is attached. The Côte du Beaune and Côte de Nuits are prime French regions. In the New World, smooth-style Pinot Noir is also made in Australia, New Zealand, and Chile.

Sangiovese

Like many red grapes, Sangiovese can be vinified in more than one style. You'll find it as a bold red as inky Brunello (page 143). But it also makes a spicy, tangy member of the smooth reds family, sustaining terrific popularity in the Tuscan blends. Sangiovese is the main grape used to make Chianti, which hails from Tuscany in central Italy. For the most reliable quality, look for Chianti labeled as "Classico," which means it has been made from the historic blend of grapes and in the classic grape-growing districts. Sangiovese is now also being made in California and Argentina on its own and blended. Despite its velvety body, the wine can taste rather tart when unblended—it has a higher acid content than many other smooth reds. But it's a great food wine, standing up beautifully to tangy tomato sauces and cutting through rich cheeses and fatty meats like a charm.

Malbec

Originally used as one of the five red Bordeaux grape varieties, Malbec is made into a smooth, dark wine in the nearby Cahors region. Malbec has come into its own today in Argentina. There, particularly in the Mendoza region, are velvety, cherry-packed wines produced to match with the local meats cooked on the grill.

Tempranillo

Tempranillo is Spain's most important red wine grape. The Rioja region, in particular, is known for Tempranillo-based red wine. There it makes wines of varying body and structure. It has hints of raspberry and strawberry fruit, and many also describe Rioja wines as leathery or dusty, which reflects both the wine's *terroir* and its oak aging. Tempranillo-based wines are also made in Portugal, California, and Argentina.

Grenache

Used extensively in the blends common in southern France, Grenache smells of ripe red fruit and lavender. It is often combined with Syrah and Mourvèdre to give the wine additional structure. Grenache is also used prolifically in Spain, there called Garnacha, and as a rosé (see Pink Wines, page 98).

Barbera

Barbera can be found in both a smooth and juicy style (see page 113). California Barberas are typically more fruit forward and fuller in body than the Italian wines.

Super-Tuscans

To thwart the restrictive governmental regulations of the day, a group of Tuscan winemakers in the 1970s began to make wines from grapes that were not officially sanctioned. Although excellent, the wines could only be labeled as "table wine" and lacked the official governmental seal of quality. The laws were changed in 1992 allowing winemakers to legally blend native Sangiovese grapes with nonnative varietals such as Merlot and Cabernet Sauvignon Today these "Super-Tuscans" are very popular in the U.S. and elsewhere.

Pappardelle with spicy lamb ragù

Choose a wine with good acidity to stand up to the tomatoes in this long-simmered meat sauce. A wine with a pronounced herbal aroma will resonate with the herbs in the dish.

2 tsp extra-virgin olive oil

1 lb ground lamb

1 yellow onion, minced

1 cup finely chopped fresh cremini mushrooms

1/4 tsp red pepper flakes, or to taste

3 cloves garlic, minced

1 3/4 cups reduced-sodium beef broth

1/4 cup dry red wine

1 cup tomato sauce

3 tbsp tomato paste

2 small fresh rosemary or thyme sprigs

1 tbsp balsamic vinegar

Kosher salt and freshly ground black pepper

3/4 lb dried pappardelle

1/4 cup freshly grated Parmesan cheese, plus more for serving

1/4 cup chopped fresh flat-leaf parsley

In a nonstick frying pan large enough to hold the sauce and the pasta, heat the oil over high heat. Add the lamb and sauté, stirring to break up any clumps, until lightly browned, about 8 minutes. Using a slotted spoon, transfer the lamb to a plate.

Pour off all but 1 tablespoon of the fat from the pan and return the pan to medium heat. Add the onion, mushrooms, and red pepper flakes and sauté until the mushrooms have released their moisture and the onion is translucent and soft, 5–7 minutes. Add the garlic and cook, stirring, until fragrant, about 1 minute.

Return the lamb to the pan and add the broth, 1/2 cup water, the wine, tomato sauce, tomato paste, and rosemary. Bring to a boil, reduce the heat to low, and simmer gently, uncovered, until the sauce has thickened slightly, 25–30 minutes. Add the vinegar and cook for 1 minute longer. Taste and season with salt and pepper. Keep warm over low heat.

About 15 minutes before the sauce is ready, bring a large pot three-fourths full of salted water to a boil. Add the pappardelle and cook until al dente, 8–10 minutes or according to the package directions.

Raise the heat under the sauce to medium. Drain the pasta, add it to the sauce, and toss and stir to combine. Add the 1/4 cup Parmesan and the parsley and again toss to combine.

Divide the pasta among warmed shallow bowls and serve right away. Pass additional Parmesan at the table.

MAKES 4 MAIN-COURSE SERVINGS

New World match

Try a Sangiovese from the Mendoza region. Less tannic than its Tuscan cousin, this Argentine red is rich in flavor, but fruity enough to handle the spicy pasta.

Old World match

A northern Italian Barbera has the natural acidity to match the tomato and to balance the richness of the lamb.

Alternative pairings

For an innovative, but delicious contrast, serve a California Blanc de Noirs (Sparkling Wines, page 39), whose refreshing mixture of fruit and fizz will nicely balance the dish.

A Sangiovese rosé (Pink Wines, page 99) has sufficient weight to marry well with the sauce, and, served well chilled, will help tame the sauce's heat.

Seared salmon with mushroom-wine sauce

Searing salmon helps it pair better with the wine, whose acidity will counter the oiliness of the fish; just be sure the wine is low in tannin. A wine with earthy aromas will link it to the mushrooms.

1 lb assorted fresh mushrooms such as shiitake, cremini, oyster, or chanterelle

3 tbsp unsalted butter

2 tbsp minced shallot

2 tbsp chopped fresh tarragon

2 tbsp chopped fresh flat-leaf parsley

Kosher salt and freshly ground black pepper

¼ cup smooth red wine

2 tsp sherry vinegar

4 skinless salmon fillets, about 6 oz each

1–2 tsp canola oil

Preheat the oven to 450°F.

Prepare the mushrooms: If using shiitake mushrooms, remove and discard the stems. Brush all the mushrooms clean, and then trim and cut them into ¾-inch pieces. This may mean keeping the small mushrooms whole.

In a large frying pan over medium-high heat, melt the butter. Add the shallot and sauté until it starts to soften, about 30 seconds. Add the mushrooms, tarragon, parsley, ½ teaspoon salt, and a few grinds of pepper and sauté until the mushrooms are soft, 2–3 minutes. Add the wine, cover, reduce the heat to low, and cook, stirring once or twice, until the mushrooms are tender, about 10 minutes. Uncover the pan and stir in the vinegar. Simmer the mixture for 1 minute longer to blend the flavors and remove from the heat.

Season the salmon on both sides with salt and pepper. Heat a large, heavy ovenproof frying pan over high heat for 2–3 minutes. Add the oil and swirl to coat the pan lightly. Place the salmon fillets, skinned side down, in the pan and sear for 2 minutes without turning. Transfer the pan to the oven and roast until the salmon is lightly firm to the touch and is opaque throughout when tested with a knife tip, about 6 minutes.

Divide the salmon evenly among warmed individual plates, and spoon the mushrooms on top or alongside, dividing evenly. Serve right away.

MAKES 4 SERVINGS

New World match

The modest tannins, good acidity, and earthy scents of a Washington State Merlot will flatter both the fish and the mushrooms.

Old World match

Choose a silky Merlot-based Bordeaux blend made near St. Emilion. The wine's herbal flavors will flatter the dish, and its smooth tannins will not overpower the fish.

Alternative pairings

A full-bodied southern French rosé based on Mourvèdre (Pink Wines, page 99) will provide nice fruit along with an acidic backbone.

Pour a bosky Pinot Noir–based Bourgogne Rouge (Juicy Reds, page 112), which has the requisite acidity to cut through the rich salmon with earthy flavors to flatter the mushrooms.

Braised chicken with mushrooms & tomatoes

Browning and then braising chicken pieces helps the mild meat form a stronger link to red wine. Choose an earthy, herbal wine with good acid to match the mushrooms, herbs, and tomatoes.

In a small bowl, combine the mushrooms and 1 cup warm water and let stand until softened, 15–20 minutes. Lift out the mushrooms and chop coarsely. Strain the soaking liquid through a fine-mesh sieve lined with cheesecloth and measure out ¼ cup. Discard the remaining liquid.

On a large plate, stir together the flour, 2 teaspoons salt, and ½ teaspoon pepper. Lightly dust the chicken thighs on all sides with the seasoned flour. In a large frying pan over high heat, warm the oil. Add the pancetta and sauté until crisp, 2–3 minutes. Transfer the pancetta to a plate. Working in 2 batches, lightly brown the chicken in the pan, turning once, 5–6 minutes total for each batch. Transfer the chicken to a platter.

Pour out all but 1 tablespoon of the fat from the pan and return to medium heat. Add the shallots and garlic and cook, stirring to scrape up the browned bits from the pan bottom, for 1 minute. Add the chopped mushrooms, pancetta, tomatoes, chicken thighs, mushroom-soaking liquid, wine, brandy, tomato paste, Worcestershire sauce, thyme, marjoram, tarragon, ¼ teaspoon salt, and ½ teaspoon pepper. Reduce the heat to low, cover, and simmer, turning the chicken pieces once. Cook until an instant-read thermometer inserted into the thickest part of the thigh, away from the bone, registers 170°F, 25–30 minutes. Remove from the heat and adjust the seasonings.

To serve, spoon some polenta onto warmed plates and top with a piece of chicken and some sauce. Garnish with the parsley. Serve right away.

MAKES 4 SERVINGS

½ oz dried porcini mushrooms

¼ cup all-purpose flour

Kosher salt and freshly ground black pepper

8 skin-on, bone-in chicken thighs

2 tbsp extra-virgin olive oil

1 slice pancetta, about ¼ inch thick, diced

⅔ cup minced shallots

2 cloves garlic, minced

3 tomatoes, peeled, seeded, and chopped

¼ cup smooth red wine

2 tbsp brandy

1 tbsp *each* tomato paste and Worcestershire sauce

1 tsp *each* dried thyme, dried marjoram, and dried tarragon

Hot cooked polenta for serving

¼ cup chopped fresh flat-leaf parsley

New World match

The many earthy flavors in an Oregon Pinot Noir will highlight the herbs, tomatoes, and mushrooms in this slow-cooked dish.

Old World match

A modest wine from Burgundy's Côte de Beaune, like a Savigny-les-Beaune, will make an ideal partner for the richly braised dark-meat chicken.

Alternative pairings

For a pleasing contrast between the wine and the food, consider a Soave Classico (Crisp Whites, page 53).

Consider an Alsatian Pinot Blanc (Soft Whites, page 69), which will be weighty enough to stand up to the dish's concentrated flavors, yet light enough to refresh the palate between bites.

Apricot-stuffed roasted pork loin

Although pork loin is mild, adding mustard and shallots and browning it well help create a match to a smooth red wine. Choose one with pronounced fruit to echo the fruits in the filling.

½ cup dried apricots, cut into ¼-inch pieces

⅓ cup raisins

3 tbsp brandy

3 tsp olive oil

½ cup thinly sliced shallots

1 tsp sherry vinegar

1 boneless center-cut pork loin roast, about 3 lb, butterflied by the butcher

1 tbsp Dijon mustard

Kosher salt and freshly ground black pepper

2 tsp cornstarch

1¾ cups reduced-sodium chicken broth

Mix together the apricots, raisins, and brandy. Let stand for 30 minutes. Drain the fruits, reserving the brandy. In a small frying pan over medium heat, warm 1 teaspoon of the oil. Add the shallots and sauté until lightly browned, 3–4 minutes. Add the vinegar, cook for 1 minute, then set aside.

Preheat the oven to 350°F. Place the pork loin, fat side down, on a cutting board. Spread the meat with the mustard and season with salt and pepper. Combine the drained fruit and shallots and spread one-half of the mixture over the center third of the meat. Fold one third of the meat over the filling. Cover the top of this third with the remaining fruit mixture, and bring the remaining third of the meat over the top of the filling to make a fat roll. Using kitchen string, tie the roll crosswise in 3 or 4 places at regular intervals, forming a compact cylinder. Then, tie a long piece of string lengthwise around the roll. Heat a large, heavy ovenproof frying pan over high heat until very hot. Add the remaining 2 teaspoons oil. Sear the pork loin fat side down until nicely browned, about 2 minutes. Turn the meat over and transfer the pan to the oven. Roast the pork until an instant-read thermometer inserted into the thickest part of the loin registers 155°–160°F, 1–1¼ hours. Transfer the meat to a cutting board and lightly tent with aluminum foil to keep warm.

Carefully spoon off as much fat as possible from the pan. Dissolve the cornstarch in 2 tablespoons of the broth. Pour the remaining broth and the reserved brandy into the pan, bring to a boil over high heat, and boil for 2–3 minutes. Gradually stir in the cornstarch mixture, and then cook, stirring, until the sauce thickens, 1–2 minutes. Season to taste with salt and pepper. To serve, carve the roast into slices ½ inch thick. Place the slices on warmed plates, spoon a little of the sauce over the meat, and serve right away. Pass the remaining sauce in a warmed bowl at the table.

MAKES 6 SERVINGS

New World match

A Pinot Noir from California's sun-drenched Sonoma Coast has the requisite fruitiness to flatter this apricot-stuffed roast.

Old World match

With its echoes of dried fruit, a quality Chianti will highlight not only the apricots and raisins, but also the nicely browned meat.

Alternative pairings

Pick a Spanish rosé Cava (Sparkling Wines, page 39) for a refreshing counterpoint to this dish's many sweet-savory elements.

Look to Burgundy for an elegant Chardonnay from Chassagne-Montrachet (Rich Whites, page 82), whose fruity, rich flavors will reference the apricots and raisins as well as the well-browned pork loin.

Pan-roasted duck breasts with dried-cherry sauce

Duck's rich meat needs an acidic wine to cut it; choose one with good cherry flavors to echo the fruit in the sauce. A fruity wine will also contrast with the sweet spices used in the rub.

1 tsp sweet paprika

1 tsp ground coriander

1 tsp Chinese five-spice powder

Kosher salt and freshly ground black pepper

4 skin-on, boneless duck breasts, 5–6 oz each

2 tsp extra-virgin olive oil

1 cup smooth red wine

1 cup reduced-sodium chicken broth

1 or 2 narrow strips orange zest, removed from the fruit with a vegetable peeler

Juice of 1 orange

2 shallots, minced

6 black peppercorns

1/2 cup dried tart cherries

1 tbsp honey

2 tbsp cold unsalted butter, cut into pieces

1 tsp cornstarch dissolved in 1 tbsp water

In a small bowl, stir together the paprika, coriander, five-spice powder, 1/2 teaspoon salt, and 1/4 teaspoon pepper to make a rub. Using a small, sharp knife, score the skin of the duck breasts in a 3/8-inch diamond pattern, being careful not to cut into the flesh. Brush the duck breasts with the oil and sprinkle the rub on both sides of each breast. Let the duck breasts stand at room temperature for 30 minutes.

Preheat the oven to 450°F. In a saucepan, combine the wine, broth, orange zest, juice, shallots, and peppercorns and bring to a boil over high heat. Reduce the heat to medium-high and cook until reduced by half, about 10 minutes. Strain the mixture through a medium-mesh sieve into a bowl; discard the contents of the sieve. Return the strained liquid to the pan, add the cherries and honey, bring to a simmer over medium heat, and simmer until the cherries are plumped, 4–5 minutes. Whisk in the butter. Gradually whisk in the cornstarch mixture and cook, stirring, until the sauce thickens, about 2 minutes. Adjust the seasonings and keep warm.

Heat a large cast-iron or heavy ovenproof frying pan over high heat until very hot. Place the breasts, skin side down, in the pan and sear until the skin is nicely browned, 3–4 minutes. Turn the breasts over and cook for 1 minute longer. Spoon the fat from the bottom of the pan and discard. Transfer the pan to the oven and roast the duck breasts until medium-rare, about 8 minutes. Remove from the oven, transfer the breasts to a cutting board, tent with aluminum foil, and let rest for 3–4 minutes.

Cut the duck breasts on the diagonal into thin slices. Fan the slices on warmed individual plates and spoon a little of the sauce over the top. Serve right away. Pass the remaining sauce in a warmed small bowl.

MAKES 4 SERVINGS

New World matches

With its intense cherry aroma, a Pinot Noir from Sonoma is a classic match for this dish.

A mouthwatering, fruity Australian Merlot, especially one from the cooler Western side of the country, will make an ideal partner for the sweetly spiced duck.

Old World match

With its spiced cherry and cranberry fruit flavors, an aged Rioja Reserva effortlessly matches the complex flavors in the sauce.

Alternative pairing

The brambly fruit and bold, tannic structure of a Napa Valley Zinfandel (Bold Reds, page 143) can easily take on the diverse tastes in this richly flavored recipe.

Osso buco

Braising veal shanks renders them meltingly tender, creating a textural match with a velvety wine. Porcini mushrooms and sweet vegetables add complexity and earthiness to the pairing.

1 oz dried porcini mushrooms

1/2 cup plus 1 tbsp all-purpose flour

Kosher salt and freshly ground black pepper

3 1/2–4 lb meaty veal shanks, cut into pieces 2 inches wide

1/3 cup extra-virgin olive oil

1 yellow onion, chopped

1 large carrot, chopped

1 celery stalk, chopped

1/4 tsp red pepper flakes, or to taste

1 3/4 cups reduced-sodium beef broth

1 can (8 oz) tomato sauce

3/4 cup smooth red wine

2 or 3 fresh thyme sprigs

1 tbsp unsalted butter, at room temperature

Chopped fresh flat-leaf parsley for garnish

In a bowl, combine the mushrooms and 1 1/2 cups warm water and let stand until softened, 15–20 minutes. Lift out the mushrooms, drain well, and chop coarsely. Strain the liquid through a fine-mesh sieve lined with cheesecloth and measure out 1 cup. Discard the remaining liquid.

Preheat the oven to 350°F. On a large plate, stir together the 1/2 cup flour, 2 teaspoons salt, and 1/2 teaspoon black pepper. Lightly dust the veal shanks on all sides with the seasoned flour. In a Dutch oven, heat the oil over medium-high heat. When the oil is hot, working in batches to avoid crowding, add the veal shanks and cook on all sides until nicely browned, about 6–8 minutes total for each batch. Transfer the shanks to a platter.

Reduce the heat to medium, add the onion, carrot, celery, and red pepper flakes, and stir to scrape up the browned bits from the pot bottom. Sauté until the vegetables start to soften, 4–5 minutes. Add the broth, tomato sauce, mushroom-soaking liquid, and wine, raise the heat to high, and bring to a boil. Add the thyme, 1/2 teaspoon kosher salt, and several grinds of black pepper. Return the veal shanks to pot, along with the mushrooms. When the liquid just returns to a boil, cover, transfer to the oven, and braise until the meat is very tender, about 2 hours. Check the pot after 1 hour to make sure the liquid is at a bare simmer and adjust the oven temperature as necessary.

Transfer the shanks to deep serving dish. In a bowl, work together the remaining 1 tablespoon flour and the butter to make a paste. Return the pot to medium heat and bring the liquid to a boil. Whisk in the paste a little at a time and cook until the sauce thickens slightly, 2–3 minutes. Spoon the sauce over the shanks, garnish with the parsley, and serve.

MAKES 6 SERVINGS

New World match

An Argentine Malbec has both the requisite tannins and ripe fruit to seamlessly match these tender veal shanks.

Old World match

A Chianti Classico will provide acidity to mirror the tomatoes in the dish and enough tannins to stand up to the meat.

A deeply colored Malbec-based Cahors from France boasts the rustic structure to handle this rich dish.

Alternative pairings

Believe it or not, a ripe, oak-aged Meursault from Burgundy (Rich Whites, page 82) has enough heft to take on the tender, roasted meat.

A hefty, Nebbiolo-based Barolo (Bold Reds, page 143) will counter the depth of the braised veal while staying true to the dish's Italian roots.

Bold reds

Intense, strong, and satisfying, bold reds have a reputation for audacious flavors. Because of their powerful attributes, these wines are best matched with assertive dishes.

Brimming with big, hearty, meaty flavors, bold reds are rich and gratifying. Cabernet Sauvignon and Zinfandel grapes are perhaps the best-known bold reds in the U.S., but nearly all the world's winemaking regions feature their own examples. The best bold wines come from hot climates where the grapes can gain full ripeness, which corresponds to high alcohol and full body in the wines made from them. Maturing in oak barrels adds more structure and aging potential to the wines. With their ripe, concentrated flavors and tannic backbone, bold reds are best paired with foods that have a certain amount of fat to stand up to them, like a richly marbled rib-eye steak or thick-cut lamb chops.

About bold reds

A dense, tannic structure and full-bodied texture dominate this style of wine. Built on big, hearty flavors, bold reds are not as immediately accessible as some of the other wine styles and, arguably, they are best appreciated as a companion to food. Nevertheless, many bold reds enjoy a cult following, especially in the New World, where the climates tend to be warmer and the wine drinkers favor stronger flavors.

Attributes of bold reds

Powerful and audacious, this style of wine can seem unappealingly dark and tannic without food to counteract its bravado. Some winemakers like to round out the flavors and textures by blending in other grapes. Bordeaux winemakers are famous for this strategy, adding velvety Merlot, meaty Malbec, and other grapes to lend softness and complexity to their Cabernet Sauvignon–based wines.

Bold red wines have some of the most unique flavors of all the wine styles. It is not uncommon for people to perceive such nuances as lead pencil, saddle, barnyard, tar, cigar box, and eucalyptus in the wines. Strange as they may seem, these flavors marry well with a variety of strong meats and pungent game dishes. Bold reds are fitting partners for cold-weather fare: slow-roasted meats or game and long-cooked braises are traditional partners. Simply grilled or panfried meats can also work well, but full-flavored cuts that have a good proportion of fat are best, as they counteract the wine's tannins. Northern Italy is famous for its full-bodied reds, which are perfect pair with egg-rich pastas topped with long-simmered meat ragùs. Bold wines with forward fruit flavors can stand up to barbecue-style sauces or mildly spiced dishes. Since many of these wines have a prominent oak flavor, they can be good matches for grilled or lightly smoked dishes.

Old Vines

In theory, the more grapevines age, the more intense their fruit—and by extension the wine made from them. This is because, as the vine ages, grape production decreases, creating increased concentration within individual grapes. If you see the words "Old Vine," "Old Clones," or "Vieilles Vignes" on a wine label, expect the wine to be even more intense in flavor, fruit, tannin, and body than a wine without such a label. Zinfandel, for one, can often be found with this designation.

1 Look

Bold wines tend to have a deep, rich red or purple color, leaning toward the brown or black end of the spectrum. They are often described as "inky," which refers both to their dense color and potent flavor.

2 Swirl

Swirl a bold red vigorously in the glass to release its powerful aromas. Typically high in alcohol, these wines will probably appear viscous and the legs will linger on the side of the glass for a long period of time.

3 Smell

Take the time to smell all of the fascinating aromas in a bold red wine, which are unique to this wine style. The aroma will change over time as the wine is exposed to air. Try to detect any scents—herbs, earth, toast—that can help you link it to the food.

4 Sip

A bold red will boast powerful flavors and dark red fruit flavors. It might taste a little furry, or chewy, which is the tannin expressing itself in the wine. Some describe the aftertaste of bold reds as meaty, even gamy, and this flavor will likely linger for a long time in your mouth. Don't be put off if the wine seems severe at first. It will soften with time and show its best qualities when paired with food.

Flavor profile

Bold reds from the Old World are likely to be more subtle and refined than their New World cousins, but it is in the New World that bold reds have really taken a foothold. There, the climate tends to be hotter and the grapes are more likely to ripen to their full extent. Consequently, New World bold reds have more pronounced fruit flavors and often more aggressive oak aromas.

Blackberry
Blackberries, black currants, and other dark fruits are very common fruity aromas perceived in bold red wines.

Cinnamon
Although the wines are not sweet, it is common for tasters to perceive nuances of sweet spices, such as those used in baking, in bold reds.

Green bell pepper
The scent of green bell peppers is a sign that a bold red wine is Cabernet Sauvignon or has another Bordeaux-style grape in the blend.

Black pepper
Peppery scents go hand-in-hand with the fruit aromas in an array of bold reds. Syrah, Zinfandel, and Petite Sirah boast healthy amounts of pepper.

Dried cherry
The concentrated flavor of dried cherries is typical in wines from warmer climates; cooler climate wines feature fresh cherry scents.

Plum
A scent reminiscent of fresh, ripe plums adds another red fruit dimension to a variety of bold reds.

Toast
A toasty aroma is the influence of the oak barrels on the wine. It is a desirable trait in bold reds, but a too-toasty wine can be a challenge to match to food.

Cigar
This is one of the more unusual but representative scents perceived in bold reds. Others include cedar, eucalyptus, and pencil shavings.

Truffle
An earthy-mushroomy-musty scent, such as you detect in a black truffle, is a common component of this category of wines.

Cloves
Along with pepper and cinnamon, pungent spices are a typical accent for bold red wines, particularly wines from warm climates.

Key bold red wines

These days, wines are being made to be consumed relatively young. Nevertheless, bold reds can benefit from some aging, which helps to mellow their tannins. Bold reds feature a high alcohol content, sometimes as much as 14 percent or more, which corresponds to a full body. They often benefit from exposure to air to soften their harsh edge; letting them breathe for an hour or more is not uncommon.

Aerating wine

Some red wines, particularly bold ones, benefit from being exposed to air to soften their tannins. One method is to open a wine an hour or two prior to drinking it, pour off a small glass, and set the bottle aside to "breathe." Another method is to pour the wine into a decanter. A young wine is poured into the vessel vigorously to provide maximum exposure to the air. An older wine is decanted slowly with the aid of a light source to separate the wine from any sediment.

Cabernet Sauvignon

Arguably the most famous red grape in the world, Cabernet Sauvignon gained fame in Bordeaux, France, where it is used as a base for many of the region's best wines. In the New World, the proliferation of Cabernet Sauvignon–based wine has helped to establish California as a top wine region with its intense, fruit-forward wine with overt oak flavors and dense tannins. Washington State is another U.S. wine region producing excellent Cabernets. There, expect the wines to be slightly less intense, due to the cooler growing climate. Chile is an up-and-coming region producing quality Cabernets in the California style. Australia, too, produces big Cabernet-based wines with concentrated fruit. Some of the best wines come from the Coonawarra region, renowned for its red soil. Whether from the Old World or the New, Cabernet Sauvignon is ideally suited to aging, which softens its hard edges and mellows its tannins. While the grape is normally thought of as a bold red, some winemakers make it into a smoother, more accessible style akin to Merlot. In general, these smooth-style Cabernets will be on the less expensive side, but consult your wine merchant to be sure.

Syrah

Winemakers make Syrah into two main types of wine: French style, based on the wines of the northern Rhône, and Australian style, called Shiraz, based on the robust, jammy wines favored by New World wine drinkers. In the northern Rhône, Syrah is the only red grape allowed by law. There, the wines have an earthy quality, dark fruit, and firm tannins. At their best, these wines are capable of extended aging. Syrah is also seen as part of the red wine blends in the southern Rhône and in the Languedoc in southwestern France. In Australia, Shiraz boasts bright, concentrated fruit layered with peppery spice. Though some believe Shiraz to be less refined and interesting than the grape's French expression, it has the advantage of being able to handle spicy foods and bolder flavors. Syrah is also popular in California where it is vinified in either style. There, wines produced in the Rhône tradition are labeled as Syrah and those made in the Australian fashion as Shiraz. Some of the distinctive aromas detected in Syrah and Syrah-based wines include "barnyard" or even "sweaty saddle," which may sound strange, but refers to the grape's pleasantly musky overtone.

Zinfandel

Zinfandel is widely planted in California. The wine is often described as "jammy," which evokes the wine's intense, concentrated fruit flavors. Zinfandel is sometimes very high in alcohol, but its tannins are not as intense as those of some other bold reds, so it is very accessible. Zinfandel also has good acidity, which creates balance in the wine. Of all the bold reds, Zinfandel pairs best with barbecue, chile, or anything with ketchup, as its fruity flavors complement or contrast nicely with grilled meats and slightly sweet sauces.

Mourvèdre

This French grape thrives in the southern Rhône region, where it is often blended with Grenache and Syrah into muscular, spice-imbued wines. The most famous wine of the region is Châteauneuf-du-Pape, but Gigondas and Vacqueyras represent some of the other flavorful blends. Just to the south lies Provence, which is famous for the Mourvèdre-based wines of the Bandol region. In Spain, you can also find single-varietal bottlings of Mourvèdre, there called Monastrell. In the New World, central and northern California are growing small quantities of Mourvèdre and making delicious wines alone or blended in the southern Rhône style.

Nebbiolo

The Nebbiolo grape makes some of the most prized wines of Italy, notably the bold reds Barolo, Barbaresco, and other fine Italian reds. The grape grows best in the fog, *nebbia* in Italian, which is common in Piedmont and is how the grape got its name. Barolo features dense, dark fruit. It can be highly tannic, but with a good amount of acidity and can age for many years age. Barbaresco is slightly less astringent and more accessible than Barolo.

Sangiovese

Known best as the primary grape in Chianti, in Tuscany, this grape also makes a very dark, tannic wine called Brunello. Brunello needs to age for several years before it is drinkable.

Petite Sirah

This grape produces huge, deeply colored wine with a spicy character. Because of its dark juice, Petite Sirah is often used in red wine blends to lend color. It is widely planted in California and South America. Some wine drinkers confuse Petite Sirah with Syrah, but they are different grapes altogether.

Quality in Bordeaux

In Bordeaux, wines are labeled according to relative quality and price, based on a rating of villages and vineyards that dates back to 1855. The best wines are labeled as "Crus Classés," or classified growths, and are grouped into up to five sub-categories. Of these, bottles labeled "Premiers Crus" are considered the top wines. Next are the wines called "Cru Bourgeois," which are still very good in quality. The remaining wines, called "Petites Chateaux," are deemed table wines.

Grilled New York steak & summer vegetables

Steak is a natural partner for red wine, but to suit this category, choose richly marbled meat. Cooking it over charcoal and being generous with the pepper will help form a stronger link.

4 New York strip steaks, each 10–12 oz and 1¼ inches thick, trimmed of excess fat

12 cremini mushrooms, or 3 large portobello mushrooms

2 yellow crookneck squashes

2 zucchini

1 large sweet onion, about 14 oz

¼ cup extra-virgin olive oil, plus more for brushing

Grated zest of 1 lemon

2 tbsp fresh lemon juice

1 large clove garlic, minced

Kosher salt and freshly ground black pepper

Remove the steaks from the refrigerator and bring to room temperature. Meanwhile, prepare a charcoal or gas grill for direct-heat cooking over medium heat.

Twist out and discard the stems from the mushrooms and brush the caps clean. With a teaspoon, scrape out the dark gills and discard. Cut the crookneck squashes and zucchini lengthwise into slices ¼ inch thick. Cut the onion crosswise into slices ½ inch thick. Push a sandwich pick or small wooden skewer through the side of each onion slice to hold the layers together as you grill. In a small bowl, whisk together the ¼ cup oil, the lemon zest and juice, garlic, ½ teaspoon salt, and a few grinds of pepper. Brush all the vegetables generously with the mixture.

Arrange the mushrooms, squashes, and onions on the grill rack and grill, turning once or twice, until tender and nicely browned, 10–12 minutes total for the mushrooms and squashes and 12–15 minutes total for the onion slices. Transfer the grilled vegetables to a plate, cover with aluminum foil, and keep warm while the steaks are cooking.

Increase the grill heat to high by turning up a gas grill or adding hot coals to a charcoal grill. Brush the steaks on both sides with olive oil, and then season on both sides with salt and pepper. Place the steaks on the grill rack and grill, turning them once about halfway through grilling, 8–10 minutes total for medium-rare, or until done to your liking. Remove the steaks from the grill and let rest for 5 minutes.

Cut the steaks into ½-inch slices, sprinkle with salt, and divide the steaks and vegetables among warmed individual plates. Serve right away.

MAKES 4 SERVINGS

New World matches

An herb-tinged Chilean Cabernet Sauvignon will highlight the vegetables as it cuts through the rich meat.

Fans of big, brooding red wines will appreciate the way a smoky Californian Petite Sirah links with well-charred beef.

Old World match

A firm, fairly tannic Bordeaux from the Haut-Médoc will have no problem standing up to the well-marbled steak.

Alternative pairing

A rosé Champagne (Sparkling Wines, page 39) might seem like an odd choice for a steak, but the wine's toastiness and rich fruit flavors are a terrific match for grilled meat.

Grilled marinated flank steak

Choose a wine with forward fruit, which will counter the saltiness and sweetness in the soy-and-brown-sugar marinade. The steak will char on the grill, linking it to a smoke-tinged wine.

New World match

Rich with the taste of ripe blackberries and cherries, a Dry Creek Zinfandel from Sonoma offers a fruity foil for the deeply marinated meat.

Old World matches

Try an Apulian Primitivo, Zinfandel's Italian cousin. Its deep dried-fruit flavors and dusty complexity flatter the sweet-savory steak.

Or, pour a spicy Syrah from France's northern Rhône to play up the meat's flavorful ginger-soy marinade.

Alternative pairing

A robust Malbec from the Mendoza (Smooth Reds, page 127) has enough muscle to handle the chewy steak.

In a small bowl, whisk together the soy sauce, oil, lemon zest and juice, garlic, ginger, and sugar to make a marinade. Place the flank steak in a shallow nonreactive pan and pour the marinade over it. Turn the steak once or twice to coat both sides evenly, and then marinate at room temperature for 30 minutes.

Prepare a charcoal or gas grill for direct-heat cooking over high heat. Place the steak on the grill rack and grill, turning once at the halfway point, for 7–8 minutes total for medium-rare, or until done to your liking. Transfer the steak to a cutting board, lightly tent with aluminum foil, and let rest for 5 minutes.

Using a sharp knife, cut the steak across the grain on the diagonal into thin slices and transfer the slices onto warmed plates. Serve right away.

MAKES 4 OR 5 SERVINGS

3 tbsp soy sauce

3 tbsp canola oil

Grated zest of 1 lemon

3 tbsp fresh lemon juice

1 clove garlic, minced

1 tsp grated fresh ginger

1 tsp firmly packed brown sugar

1 flank steak, about 1½ lb, trimmed

Braised short ribs with mashed potatoes

Braising on the bone gives a rich quality to beef, helping it contend with the full flavors of the wine. Buttermilk and horseradish in the potatoes lend a tangy counterpoint to the partnership.

1/3 cup all-purpose flour

Kosher salt and freshly ground black pepper

4 lb English-cut beef short ribs, cut into 3-inch pieces

3 tbsp extra-virgin olive oil

1 yellow onion, chopped

1 carrot, chopped

1 celery stalk, chopped

1 parsnip, peeled and chopped

4 cloves garlic

2 1/2 cups reduced-sodium beef broth

1 cup bold red wine

2 tbsp balsamic vinegar

2 tbsp tomato paste

4 or 5 fresh thyme sprigs

1 bay leaf

2 lb Yukon gold potatoes, peeled and cut into halves

1/2 cup unsalted butter

2 tbsp prepared horseradish

1 cup buttermilk, warmed

Preheat the oven to 325°F. On a large plate, stir together the flour, 1 teaspoon salt, and a few grinds of pepper. Lightly dust the short ribs on both sides with the seasoned flour. In a Dutch oven, heat the oil over high heat. When the oil is almost smoking, working in batches, add the short ribs and sear, turning once, until nicely browned on both sides, 3–4 minutes total for each batch. Transfer the ribs to a platter.

Pour off all but 2 tablespoons of the fat from the pot and return to medium-low heat. Add the onion, carrot, celery, parsnip, and garlic and stir to scrape up the browned bits from the pot bottom. Sauté the vegetables until they begin to soften, 3–4 minutes. Return the short ribs to the pot and add the broth, wine, vinegar, tomato paste, thyme, and bay leaf. Raise the heat to high, bring to a boil, cover, and transfer the pot to the oven. Braise until the meat is very tender, 2–2 1/2 hours.

About 30 minutes before the ribs are ready, prepare the potatoes. In a saucepan, combine the potatoes with salted water to cover and bring to a boil over high heat. Reduce heat to low and simmer, partially covered, until the potatoes are tender, about 20 minutes. Drain the potatoes and pass through ricer into a bowl. Gradually mix in the butter, then the horseradish, and finally the buttermilk, stirring vigorously until creamy. Season with salt and pepper. Spoon into a warmed bowl and keep warm.

Transfer the ribs to a platter and keep warm. Strain the liquid from the pot through a fine-mesh sieve in a large glass measuring cup. Using the back of a spoon, press firmly against the vegetables to extract as much flavor as possible. Discard the contents of the sieve. Spoon off and discard the surface fat, then pour the liquid over the ribs. Divide the ribs and potatoes among warmed shallow bowls and serve right away.

MAKES 4 SERVINGS

New World match

A Petite Sirah from California is anything but meek. Inky-dark in the glass, the ultraripe flavors and full-bodied style make it a perfect partner for these rich-tasting ribs.

Old World matches

With ample tannins courtesy of its thick-skinned Nebbiolo grapes, Barolo from Piedmont would also work well with the braised meat.

Amarone, an amped-up version of a Valpolicella (see Juicy Reds, page 113), will match the richness of the short ribs.

Alternative pairing

The deep flavors of an old-vine Spanish Garnacha from Priorat (Smooth Reds, page 127) mirror those found in this long-cooked dish.

Herb-crusted lamb chops with celery root gratin

Rich meat with a moderate amount of fat counters the tannins in a weighty wine. Choose a wine with pronounced herbal aromas to mirror the fresh herbs that cloak the lamb.

4 tbsp unsalted butter

4 tbsp extra-virgin olive oil

1 large yellow onion, about 1/2 lb, thinly sliced

Kosher salt and freshly ground black pepper

4 large Yukon gold potatoes, about 2 lb total weight, peeled and cut into slices 1/8 inch thick

1 celery root, about 1 lb, peeled and cut into slices 1/8 inch thick

1/3 cup dry white wine

About 1/3 cup reduced-sodium chicken broth

1/3 cup heavy cream

12 lamb rib chops, 3 1/2–4 lb total weight, each about 1 1/2 inches thick, trimmed

1/2 cup minced mixed fresh herbs such as flat-leaf parsley, thyme, mint, marjoram, and rosemary

1 tbsp Dijon mustard

2 cloves garlic, finely chopped

Preheat the oven to 375°F. Generously butter a small oval baking dish with 2 tablespoons of the butter. In a large frying pan over low heat, warm 2 tablespoons of the oil. Add the onion and sauté until lightly browned, 8–10 minutes. Distribute half of the onion slices in the prepared dish and sprinkle with a little salt and pepper. Top with a layer of potato and celery root slices, slightly overlapping, and season again. Repeat the layers with the remaining vegetables, seasoning each layer.

In a saucepan over medium-high heat, combine the wine, 1/3 cup broth, and the cream and bring almost to a boil. Carefully pour the hot liquid evenly over the vegetables. Add more broth as needed so the liquid comes halfway up the sides of the dish. Dot the top with bits of the remaining 2 tablespoons butter. Cover the dish with aluminum foil, place in the oven, and bake for 30 minutes. Remove the foil, push down on the vegetables with a spatula, and continue to bake, uncovered, until the vegetables are tender when pierced with a knife tip, about 30 minutes longer. Re-cover the dish with aluminum foil and let the gratin stand for 15–20 minutes.

Raise the oven temperature to 450°F. Season the lamb chops on both sides with salt and pepper. Stir together the remaining 2 tablespoons olive oil, the herbs, mustard, and garlic. Spread the herb mixture on both sides of the chops. Place an oiled flat rack in a large roasting pan. Arrange the lamb chops on the rack and roast until an instant-read thermometer inserted into the thickest part of a chop away from bone registers 135°F for medium-rare, 15–17 minutes. Remove from the oven, lightly tent the chops with aluminum foil, and let rest for 5 minutes.

For each serving, arrange 2 chops and a spoonful of the gratin on a warmed plate. Serve right away.

MAKES 6 SERVINGS

New World match

Try a sun-dappled Syrah from California's Central Coast. Its earthy mix of red fruit flavors and fresh-ground spices will link with both the chops and the gratin.

Old World match

Choose a Syrah from Crozes-Hermitage in France's northern Rhône for a smoky, peppery counterpoint to the gaminess of the lamb chops.

Alternative pairings

Serve an herbal, Malbec-based Cahors from France (Smooth Reds, page 127), which will match well with the herb-crusted lamb.

With its slightly chewy tannins, a Chilean Merlot (Smooth Reds, page 126) will mimic the tender texture of the lamb.

Lamb kebabs with spiced rice pilaf

Green bell peppers, fresh rosemary, and black peppercorns are all common aromas found in bold red wines, which, coupled with rich lamb, create an effortless aromatic complement.

In an electric spice grinder, combine the fennel seeds, peppercorns, and 1/2 teaspoon salt and grind finely. In a bowl, whisk together the ground spices, 2 tablespoons olive oil, the lemon juice, garlic, and rosemary. Place the lamb in a bowl, sprinkle with the spice mixture, and toss until the meat is evenly coated with the seasonings. Cover and refrigerate for 2–3 hours. Remove from the refrigerator about 30 minutes before grilling.

Place the rice in a bowl and rinse repeatedly in cold water until the water runs clear. Cover the rice with clear water and let soak for 15 minutes. Meanwhile, in a saucepan over medium heat, melt the butter. Add the onion and a pinch of salt and sauté the onion until translucent, about 5 minutes. Add the garlic and sauté until fragrant, about 1 minute. Drain the rice through a sieve, add the rice to the saucepan, and stir for 1–2 minutes to coat well with the onion mixture. Add the saffron threads, cinnamon, apricots, and a little salt and pepper. Pour in the broth, cover tightly, and bring to a boil over high heat. Reduce the heat to very low and cook until the liquid is absorbed and the rice is tender, about 18 minutes.

Meanwhile, prepare a charcoal or gas grill for direct-heat cooking over high heat. Thread the lamb and pepper pieces alternately onto soaked bamboo or metal skewers. Place the skewers on the grill rack and grill, turning once about halfway through grilling, until the bell pepper is lightly charred and the lamb is nicely browned on both sides, 8–10 minutes total for medium-rare, or until done to your liking. Remove from the grill.

When the rice is done, remove it from the heat and let stand, covered, for 5 minutes. Uncover the rice and fluff with a fork, removing and discarding the cinnamon stick. Divide the rice among warmed individual plates, top with the kebabs, and serve right away.

MAKES 4 SERVINGS

1/2 tsp fennel seeds

1/2 tsp black peppercorns

Kosher salt

4 tbsp extra-virgin olive oil

2 tbsp fresh lemon juice

1 clove garlic, minced

1 tsp minced fresh rosemary

1 1/4 lb lamb leg meat, cut into 1 1/2-inch cubes

1 cup basmati or other long-grain white rice

1 tbsp unsalted butter

1 small yellow onion, finely chopped

1 clove garlic, minced

Pinch of saffron threads

1/2 cinnamon stick

1/4 cup diced dried apricots

Freshly ground pepper

1 1/2 cups reduced-sodium chicken broth

1 large green bell pepper, seeded and cut into 2-inch squares

New World match
A big Napa Valley Cabernet Sauvignon will complement these meaty skewers and echo the scent of the bell pepper.

An Argentine Cabernet Sauvignon has just the right touch of herbaceousness to bring out the green pepper and fennel flavors of the dish.

Old World match
A Monastrell (also known as Mourvèdre) from central Spain boasts peppery flavors that warmly reference the dish's Middle Eastern seasonings.

Alternative pairing
A barrel-aged Pinot Noir from Willamette Valley, Oregon (Smooth Reds, page 126) will provide the smoky flavors and underlying spiciness to stand up to similar flavors in the lamb.

Moroccan lamb tagine with olives & chickpeas

The assertive flavor of a bold red counteracts the exotic spices in this dish. A final sprinkle of cilantro helps the dish match better to a wine with pronounced herbal flavors.

1 tsp ground ginger

Kosher salt and freshly ground black pepper

1 tsp *each* mild smoked Spanish paprika, ground cinnamon, cayenne pepper, and ground cumin

1/4 tsp saffron threads

3 cloves garlic, minced

1/2 cup chopped onion

4 tbsp extra-virgin olive oil

3 lb bone-in lamb shoulder stew meat

1 can (14 1/2 oz) diced tomatoes with juice

1 can (11 1/2 oz) vegetable juice such as V-8 juice

1 3/4 cups reduced-sodium beef broth

1/2 cup coarsely chopped pitted Kalamata olives

1/4 cup raisins

1 tbsp honey

1 can (14 1/2 oz) chickpeas

2 cups hot cooked couscous

Chopped fresh cilantro

Preheat the oven to 325°F.

In a spice grinder, combine the ginger, 1 teaspoon salt, 1 teaspoon black pepper, the paprika, cinnamon, cayenne pepper, cumin, and saffron and pulse 2 or 3 times to blend. Add the garlic, onion, and 2 tablespoons of the oil and process until a coarse paste forms. In a Dutch oven, heat the remaining 2 tablespoons oil over medium heat. Add the spice paste and sauté until fragrant, 2–3 minutes. Reduce the heat to medium-low, add the lamb, and stir to coat the meat with the spice mixture. Cook for 2–3 minutes to blend the flavors.

Add the tomatoes, vegetable juice, broth, olives, raisins, and honey to the pan. Raise the heat to medium-high, bring to a boil, cover, and place in the oven. Braise the lamb until very tender and the meat falls easily from the bone, about 2 hours. Remove from the oven and transfer the lamb to a platter. When the lamb is cool enough to handle, remove any bones and discard. Using a large spoon, skim off as much fat as possible from the sauce in the pot and return the lamb to the sauce.

Drain and rinse the chickpeas, then add them to the lamb and sauce. Return the pot, uncovered, to the oven. Braise until all the elements are heated through and the sauce is bubbling, about 30 minutes.

Divide the couscous among warmed plates and top with the lamb. Garnish with the cilantro and serve right away.

MAKES 4 SERVINGS

New World match

The robust fruit and pepper flavors of an Australian Shiraz from the McLaren Vale region create a savory backdrop for the exotic spices in this classic dish.

Old World match

Look to Barolo's refined cousin, Barbaresco, for an elegant match that drapes the dish's many elements with its modestly tannic cloak.

Alternative pairings

If you prize subtlety over strength, pour a Rioja Gran Reserva (Smooth Reds, page 127). Its quiet fruit and oak dimension will gently frame the long-simmering lamb.

Turn to Chile for an herb-scented Carmenère (similar to Merlot; Smooth Reds, page 126) to bring out the flavor of the olives and chickpeas.

Sweet wines

Fragrant, luscious, and syrupy, sweet wines boast an array of complex flavors. Far from cloying, they are balanced by a brisk acidity, making them the perfect end to any meal.

The lush, aromatic flavor of a good dessert wine is unmistakable. Superb examples are made all over the world, including Sauternes from France and Vin Santo from Italy. Port, a fortified sweet wine, is another popular example from Portugal. Some of the best sweet wines are made from grapes that are allowed to remain on the vine long past the usual harvest time, which concentrates their flavors. Some are affected by a beneficial mold, which further focuses the flavors and lends a mysterious but pleasing musty nuance to the wine. Often high in alcohol, sweet wines are usually consumed after dinner with strong cheeses or as companions to dessert.

About sweet wines

With a wide range of flavors, sweet whites are one of the most varied categories. Despite their sugary nature, good dessert wines will not taste overly sweet, as they are offset by a healthy amount of acid. Sweet wines are the perfect partner for many types of desserts, and they are apt companions for strong cheeses, tempering their harsh edges. Some aficionados also enjoy sweet wines paired with foie gras.

Noble rot

This term refers to *Botrytis cinerea,* a fungus that attacks ripe white grapes and, if the weather conditions are right, dries them out, resulting in intensely concentrated sweet grapes and a faintly musty flavor. The mold does not occur every year, nor does it spread evenly through a vineyard, and careful handpicking is necessary. All this leads to some of the world's great dessert wines, such as French Sauternes, select German Rieslings, and a handful of wines from North America, which can be pricey.

Attributes of sweet wines

Many sweet wines are labeled "late-harvest," which means the grapes are picked several days, sometimes even weeks, after the normal harvest is finished. During this time the grapes become exceedingly sweet as their natural sugars concentrate. When making the wine, fermentation is stopped before all the sugar is converted to alcohol, leaving behind a sweet impression. In the case of Port, a small amount of brandy is added to the wine to kill the yeasts and stop fermentation before all the natural grape sugar has been consumed by the yeast. In order to balance their intense flavors, sweet wines need a good amount of acid. The cool climactic conditions that produce some of the best dessert wines in the world are also perfect for encouraging the growth of "noble rot," a prized mold that dries out the grapes while still on the vine and lends a wonderful, mysterious flavor to the finished wine.

When pairing sweet wines with food, look to the relative smell of the wine to dictate what is served with it. Apricot-scented wines pair well with desserts featuring nuts, caramel, or honey. Almond- or orange-scented wines go well with desserts based on apples or pears. Wines with berry or nutty aromas can pair well with chocolate. But the most important thing to remember when pairing sweet wines with food is that the wine should be at least as sweet as the food served with it.

1 Look

The color of a sweet wine reflects its richness, from deep gold, to amber-orange, to tawny brown. Some fortified sweet wines, like Port, are dark red, purple, or brown. The lighter the color of the wine, the less intense the flavor will likely be. A darker color usually means an older wine.

2 Swirl

Most sweet wines won't so much swirl in the glass as slosh. Treat them gently and notice the thick, lingering legs on the side of the glass. Though it may look like syrup—and indeed will taste syrupy—the wine's viscous texture has more to do with its high alcohol and sugar content than its flavor.

3 Smell

Sweet wines boast alluring fruity aromas, including dried stone fruits, candied citrus, and dried berries. Toasty, nutty, and floral essences are also common.

4 Sip

Although the flavors of sweet wines will differ, sometimes dramatically, they share an intense sweetness that is tempered by a good dose of pleasing acidity. Richly textured, dessert wines will fill the mouth and coat it, and the flavor will linger on the tongue for a long period of time.

Flavor profile

Sweet wines from the Old World have a long history and are crafted with great richness, structure, and balance. Sweet wines from the New World tend to be softer, a bit sweeter, and less complex than those from the Old World. Fortified wines are mostly seen in Old-World regions, but some New World winemakers are beginning to make delicious Port-style wines from native grapes.

Floral

Cool-climate white grapes, such as Riesling and Gewürztraminer, feature a variety of perfume-like floral essences.

Caramel

A flavor like that of caramel is often found in oak-aged dessert wines, such as tawny Port.

Dried apricot

The apricot aromas typical in many soft white grapes become even more concentrated when presented in sweet wines.

Pineapple

The pineapple-like qualities of Sauvignon Blanc and Gewürztraminer grapes become even more pronounced in late-harvest wines.

Prune

A plum-scented wine transforms into a prune-scented wine when made in a sweet or fortified style.

Pear

A number of sweet wines feature soft, honeyed, tree fruit aromas, like you find in ripe pears.

Fig

The flavor and aroma of sweet, ripe figs is another fruit often associated with sweet wines.

Chocolate

Aging in oak helps give some Ports a chocolatey scent and taste. Wines with a strong flavor of chocolate will pair best with chocolate desserts.

Honey

The impression of honey in sweet wines comes from both the sugary flavor and unctous texture of the wine.

Hazelnut

Look for a hazelnut flavor in Port-style fortified wines, particularly tawny Ports. A nutty aroma is also likely in Vin Santo.

Key sweet wines

In sweet wines, the percentage of alcohol can range from as little as 6 percent to more than 16 percent, but the higher-alcohol wines have superior aging capability. To determine whether or not a wine is sweet, look for clues such as "late harvest," "late-picked," or *"recioto"* on the wine label. Sweet wines are usually consumed in smaller quantities than dry wines, and they are often available in half bottles.

Eiswein

Eiswein is a German and Austrian term for wine made from grapes left on the vine long after the typical autumn harvest and into winter. When the grapes freeze, it causes their natural sugars to concentrate, resulting in an intensely sweet but high-acid wine. Eiswein is rare, since the right conditions for making it do not occur every year. It is also made in North America, particularly in Ontario, Canada, and the Finger Lakes region of New York State; there it is called "ice wine."

Semillon

Semillon forms the basis for Sauternes, one of the most prized dessert wines in the world. For this wine, both Semillon and Sauvignon Blanc grapes are left on the vine well past the normal harvesting time to concentrate their sugars. Sauternes is only made in years when the beneficial fungus *botrytis cinerea,* or noble rot (see page 154) affects the grapes, lending its musty flavor to the wine. This scarcity causes the price to be rather high. Other late-harvest Semillon-based wines are found in Bordeaux, such as Barsac, and in the New World in California and Australia.

Riesling

The great dessert wines of Germany are based on the Riesling grape. Look for Rieslings labeled *Auslese,* indicating the wine is made from select bunches of very ripe grapes; *Beerenauslese,* signifying a sweeter wine made from overripe, concentrated grapes that have been individually harvested; or ultrasweet *Trockenbeerenauslese,* which means the grapes are both individually harvested and affected by noble rot. Late-harvest Rieslings are also produced in neighboring Alsace, France, as well as in the New World in cool climes of the United States and Australia.

Muscat

The Muscat grape makes pleasantly sweet wines, some which are fortified, notably from France and Italy in the Old World and California and Australia in the New World. Muscat can be found in a refreshingly low-alcohol sparkling form in Asti in Northern Italy, where it is called Moscato d'Asti.

Gewürztraminer

Late-harvest Gewürztraminer grapes make world-class dessert wines imbued with the grape's distinctive spice. In the old world, look for these wines in Germany with the same classifications as the Riesling-based wines (see above). Look for them also in Alsace and in cool-climate regions of the New World.

Sauvignon Blanc

Late-harvest Sauvignon Blanc grapes are typically blended with Semillon to make the highly prized dessert wines of Sauternes and neighboring villages in Bordeaux, France. They can also be found bottled as single-varietal wines in the New World.

Vin Santo

Made in central Italy, Vin Santo, literally "holy wine," is considered one of the world's great dessert wines. Made from Trebbiano and Malvasia grapes that have been dried on straw mats, the wine is fermented in small barrels and aged for several years. The resulting wine has a nutty flavor with concentrated fruit.

Chenin Blanc

The cool climate of France's Loire valley is the perfect environment for making dessert wines from superripe Chenin Blanc grapes. Perhaps the best known come from Vouvray and are labelled *moelleux.*

Ruby Port

Blended from a variety of young wines that are produced in nonvintage years, this style of Port is left in the barrel for just two to three years, after which it still retains the juicy, fruity flavor of the original wine. As its name suggests, the wine boasts a deep red color and pleasing fruity flavors, despite its high alcohol content. A Port labeled "Vintage Character" indicates a step up in quality, but not at the level of true vintage Port (see right). Look for the words "Porto" or "Oporto" on the label to indicate that the wine is authentic. Port-style wines are also being made in the New World.

Tawny Port

This style of Port is blended from wines of many vintages. It is aged for many years before bottling, which helps develop the characteristic deep, lingering nutty flavor and caramel color. Tawny ports can be expensive, especially those that are aged for long periods of time, which enhances their rich, creamy, and nutty qualities. However, you can get good quality from Ports that have been aged for as little as ten years. Unlike most other dessert wines, Port is best served at room temperature rather than cold. Look for Port-style wines from the U.S. and in Australia as well.

Vintage Port

Expensive and hard to come by, vintage Port is made only in certain years when the producer deems the harvest an exceptional one. Unlike ruby and tawny Port, vintage Port is released after only a few years of aging, after which it needs extensive time in a cellar—up to 20 years is not uncommon—in order to mellow its forceful tannins and potent flavors. These wines also demand careful decanting to separate them from the sediment that forms in the bottle during the long aging process.

Panna cotta with fresh mango

Lightly sweetened, this dessert will not compete with the sweetness of the wine. Its rich mouthfeel complements a lush dessert wine or contrasts with a light, even spritzy one.

2 tsp unflavored gelatin

1 cup half-and-half

½ cup sugar

Grated zest of 1 orange

1¾ cups heavy cream

1 tsp vanilla extract

Pinch of kosher salt

1 ripe mango, peeled, pitted, and diced

Sliced mango for garnish

In a small saucepan, sprinkle the gelatin over the half-and-half and let the gelatin soften for 5 minutes, stirring occasionally. Add the sugar and the orange zest. Place the pan over medium-low heat and warm, stirring occasionally, just until the sugar dissolves and a few small bubbles appear around the edges of the pan, about 4 minutes. Do not let the mixture boil. Remove from the heat and pour in the heavy cream. Strain the mixture through a fine-mesh sieve into a glass measuring cup. Add the vanilla extract and salt and mix well.

Divide the mango among six ½ cup ramekins. Slowly pour the gelatin mixture into the ramekins, dividing it evenly. Cover the ramekins with plastic wrap and refrigerate until set, at least 4 hours.

The panna cotta can be served in the ramekins or unmolded. If unmolding, have ready a bowl of hot water. One at a time, run a thin-bladed knife along the edge of each mold to loosen it from the ramekin sides. Dip the ramekin about halfway into the hot water for a few seconds, then dry the bottom on a towel. Invert a dessert plate on top of the ramekin, and quickly invert the ramekin and plate together, lightly shaking the ramekin to help release the panna cotta. Garnish the plates with mango slices and serve right away.

MAKES 6 SERVINGS

New World match

The heady blend of exotic fruit flavors in a California Late-harvest Gewürztraminer make it an ideal match for this tropical fruit dessert.

Old World matches

A Moscato d'Asti's gentle fizz and peachy flavors will flatter the mango and cut through the cream.

Brachetto d'Acqui, a lightly sparkling red Italian dessert wine, will be a nice foil to the rich panna cotta.

Alternative pairing

An extra-dry Prosecco (Sparkling Wines, page 39), with its abundant fruit and suggestion of sweetness, will push the panna cotta in a savory direction.

Wine-poached pears

For this recipe you can change the wine that's used to poach the pears based on what you want to serve with them. Orange- or apricot-scented wines are a nice complement to the fruit.

Select a saucepan just large enough to hold the pears. Cut out a circle of parchment paper to fit just inside the pan.

One at a time, peel the pears, leaving the stem intact. Using a small melon baller or grapefruit spoon, and working from the blossom end, scoop out and discard the core. Cut a thin slice from the bottom so the pear will stand upright. Repeat with the remaining pears.

In the saucepan, combine the wine, orange zest, sugar, cinnamon stick, peppercorns, and allspice, and bring to a boil over high heat. Reduce the heat to low and simmer for 5 minutes to blend the flavors.

Gently lower the pears into the simmering liquid, either standing them upright or laying them on their sides. Place the parchment circle lightly on top of the pears and simmer them until they are translucent and a knife tip slips in easily, 15–18 minutes. Using a slotted spoon, carefully transfer the pears to a bowl.

Bring the poaching liquid to a boil over high heat and boil until reduced to ¾ cup, about 15 minutes. Strain the liquid through a fine-mesh sieve into a bowl. Discard the contents of the sieve. Let the syrup cool for 5–10 minutes, and then pour it over the pears. When the pears and syrup are completely cool, cover and refrigerate until well chilled, for at least several hours or up to overnight.

Stand the pears in individual dessert bowls and spoon the syrup over the top. Garnish each serving with a mint sprig and accompany with a cookie, if desired. Serve right away.

MAKES 4 SERVINGS

4 small, firm Bosc pears

1 bottle (750 ml) sweet wine

Zest of 1 orange, removed in 1 or 2 narrow strips with a vegetable peeler

2 tbsp sugar

½ cinnamon stick

5 or 6 black peppercorns

2 or 3 whole allspice

Fresh mint sprigs

Small, crisp cookies for serving, optional

New World matches

For a sweet complement, serve the poached fruit with a Canadian ice wine made from pear-scented Riesling grapes.

A late-harvest Gewürz-traminer from California or the Pacific Northwest plays off the pear's straightforward flavor with a pleasing blend of pungence and ripe fruit aromas.

Old World matches

Grab two bottles of a fortified French Muscat from the Rhone or Languedoc-Roussillon. Use one to poach the pears and the other to savor with the gently spiced fruit.

A ruby Port's raisiny sweetness and clove-studded bouquet will deliciously echo the spices in the sauce.

Pecan-nectarine strudel

This match is multilayered: the dessert's richness is cut by the wine's acid; dried fruits and chocolate both complement and contrast the wine's fruitiness; the nuts complement oak flavors.

⅓ cup diced dried nectarines, apricots, or peaches

⅓ cup golden raisins

1 tbsp brandy

½ cup whole-milk ricotta cheese

¼ cup miniature semisweet chocolate chips or chopped semisweet chocolate

2 tbsp honey

1 tsp grated orange zest

¼ tsp ground allspice

¼ tsp kosher salt

Pinch of freshly ground black pepper

1½ cups unsalted butter, melted and cooled

5 sheets filo dough, thawed according to package directions

¾ cup finely chopped pecans

2 tsp granulated sugar

Confectioners' sugar for garnish

In a small bowl, stir together the nectarines, raisins, and brandy. Let stand for a few minutes. In another bowl, whisk the ricotta cheese until it is smooth and creamy. Add the fruits and brandy, chocolate chips, honey, orange zest, allspice, salt, and pepper and mix well; set aside.

Preheat the oven to 350°F. Cut a sheet of parchment paper to fit the bottom of a 12-by-16-inch rimmed baking sheet.

Place the parchment paper, a long side facing you, on a work surface and lightly brush it with melted butter. Place 1 sheet of filo on the buttered parchment paper, and lightly brush it with the butter. (As you work with the filo, keep the unused sheets covered with a barely damp towel). Sprinkle the filo evenly with about 2 tablespoons pecans. Top with a second filo sheet, brush it with butter, and sprinkle with about 2 tablespoons pecans. Repeat with 3 more filo sheets, buttering each one and using the remaining nuts. Sprinkle each of the last 2 layers with 1 teaspoon granulated sugar in addition to the nuts. Spoon the ricotta mixture in a strip down the near long side of the filo, positioning it about 2 inches away from the edge and stopping 2 inches from the right and left edges. Using the parchment paper for support, roll the long uncovered edge of the filo up over the filling into a compact log. Pinch the ends together. Lift the parchment paper and the strudel roll onto the baking sheet. Brush the top and sides with butter.

Bake the strudel until it is crisp and lightly browned, 35–40 minutes. Remove from the oven and let cool on the pan on a rack for 20 minutes. Using a serrated knife, trim off the pinched ends, then cut the strudel into 8 equal-sized pieces and place on dessert plates. Using a fine-mesh sieve, dust the slices with the confectioners' sugar and serve.

MAKES 8 SERVINGS

New World matches

A honeyed late-harvest Australian Semillon neatly references both the brandied fruit and citrus zest in this multi-layered dessert.

The stone-fruit flavors and bracing acidity of an unctuous late-harvest Argentinian Torrontes (similar to Sauvignon Blanc) make it an ideal partner to just about any dessert made with nectarines.

Old World matches

The toasted nut and apricot flavors of a Tuscan Vin Santo are perfect with this pecan-studded fruit strudel.

With flavors ranging from mocha to rum raisin, a ten-year old Tawny Port has the requisite complexity to accompany this highly nuanced pastry.

Tarte Tatin

The caramel flavors in this tart set off wines with oak flavors, while the dessert's richness is tempered by the wine's acid. If you choose a wine on the lighter side, omit the crème fraîche.

6 tbsp unsalted butter

²/₃ cup sugar

Pinch of kosher salt

3 lb Golden Delicious apples, peeled, quartered, and cored

1 sheet frozen puff pastry, 8 oz, thawed according to package directions

Crème fraîche or lightly sweetened whipped cream for serving, optional

Preheat the oven to 375°F. In a 10-inch ovenproof frying pan over medium heat, melt the butter. Add the sugar and cook until the sugar turns light amber, about 5 minutes. Remove from the heat and add the salt. Arrange the apple wedges on one of their cut sides in the pan, forming a tight, almost overlapping circle around the edges, and then fill the center with the remaining wedges.

Return the pan to high heat and cook until the sugar and juices turn deep amber, about 10 minutes. Remove from the heat and, with tongs or a knife tip, turn the apple wedges to their other cut side. Return the pan to high heat and continue to cook until the second sides of the wedges turn golden brown, about 5 minutes longer.

While the apples are cooking, roll out the pastry on a sheet of parchment paper into a round 11 inches in diameter. Using a 10-inch plate as a guide, trim the pastry into a 10-inch round. Transfer the pastry on the parchment to the refrigerator until you are ready to bake the tart.

When the apples are ready, remove the pan from the heat. Carefully flip the puff pastry onto the apples and lift off the parchment paper. Gently tuck the pastry down around the edges of the apples. With a small knife, cut four 1-inch slits into the pastry to release steam during baking.

Bake until the crust is puffed and golden brown, about 30 minutes. Remove the tart from the oven and let rest for 15 minutes. Invert a large, flat platter on top of the frying pan, then carefully invert the platter and the pan together. Lift off the pan, releasing the tart onto the platter. Cut the tart into wedges and serve warm, topped with crème fraîche, if using.

MAKES 8 SERVINGS

New World matches

Lighter than their Portuguese cousins, toffee-scented Australian tawny Ports make tasty partners for caramel-flavored desserts.

Marked by butterscotch and baked-apple aromas, Australian fortified Muscats match a variety of fruit-based desserts.

Old World matches

An apple-kissed French Sauternes or Barsac is a classic partner for this dessert, one of France's best-loved sweets.

For a less alcoholic and more refreshing match, try a late-harvest *Auslese* Riesling. The wine's natural acidity will help temper the sweetness of both the wine and the caramel.

Warm chocolate cakes with raspberry sauce

Thanks to their bright flavor and acidity, the addition of berries helps connect a wine with cherry or berry nuances to chocolate desserts. Fortified wines are a perfect match.

1 package frozen sweetened raspberries, thawed

Butter and all-purpose flour for preparing the ramekins

6 tbsp unsalted butter, cut into 6 to 8 pieces

6 oz bittersweet chocolate, chopped

3 eggs

1/3 cup sugar

1 tsp vanilla extract

1/4 tsp kosher salt

2 tbsp all-purpose flour

In a food processor, process the raspberries until smooth. Place a fine-mesh sieve over a bowl and pour the puréed raspberries through the sieve. Using the back of a large spoon, press firmly against the purée to extract as much liquid as possible. Cover the raspberry sauce and refrigerate until ready to use. Discard the contents of the sieve.

Preheat the oven to 400°F. Generously butter six 3/4-cup ramekins, then dust with flour, tapping out the excess. Place the ramekins on a rimmed baking sheet to support them in the oven.

Combine the 6 tablespoons butter and chocolate in a heatproof bowl and place over (not touching) barely simmering water in a saucepan. As the chocolate and butter melt, stir them occasionally. When they are fully melted, remove from over the heat and stir until blended. Let the chocolate-butter mixture stand for a few minutes to cool slightly.

In a bowl, using a mixer fitted with the whip attachment, beat together the eggs and sugar on medium speed until light and fluffy, 3–4 minutes. Add the vanilla and salt and beat until incorporated. Using a rubber spatula, fold the flour and the chocolate mixture into the egg mixture just until the chocolate is incorporated. Spoon the batter into the prepared ramekins, dividing it evenly. Bake the cakes until nicely puffed and slightly firm to the touch, 12–13 minutes.

Remove the cakes from the oven and let cool for 5 minutes. With a small spoon, make a little hole in the top of each cake and pour about 2 teaspoons of the raspberry sauce into the hole. Serve the cakes warm, passing the remaining raspberry sauce in a small bowl at the table.

MAKES 6 SERVINGS

New World matches

A fortified red made from berry-kissed Black Muscat grapes will sweetly flatter both the cake and the sauce.

The concentrated berry flavors of a late-harvest Zinfandel from California will highlight the sauce, amplifying its acidic contrast to the bittersweet cake.

Old World matches

Warm cake meets warming wine when you pour a ruby Port, with its amped-up alcohol and cocoa-friendly flavors.

For a rustic match to the cake's bittersweet flavors, serve a Banyuls, simliar to Port, from France's Languedoc-Roussillon region.

Menus

The following wine-and-food pairing menus feature multiple courses and multiple wines. Use the suggestions here, or create your own combinations using the guidelines below.

When creating a menu of recipes matched with wine, conventional wisdom tells us to progress from lighter to heavier foods and wines, beginning with whites, progressing to reds, and ending with sweet wines. While this thinking works quite well, don't feel hampered by it. There are many exceptions to this rule. For example, people who enjoy foie gras as a first course often pair it with Sauternes, a sweet wine, and follow with a dry wine. A juicy red might be the perfect accompaniment to an appetizer that is followed by a rich white paired with an indulgent poultry or veal dish. The choice, really, is up to you.

When planning the food and wine matches, keep in mind the seasons, the ethnic origin of the dishes, or the style of the occasion. For example, a springtime dinner suggests crisp wines to go with the season's light fare, while a party in the wintertime evokes heartier, warming foods and matching wines. On the other hand, a menu based on Spanish foods might call for a Cava, Albariño, or Rioja while Italian-inspired meal brings to mind Pinot Grigio, Dolcetto, or Barbaresco. If you are hosting a casual meal, a rustic table wine will do just fine, while a special-occasion might suggest finer, more nuanced wines and refined dishes. You can also create a menu based on different expressions of the same wine, as in the sparkling wine menu above.

Summertime Dinner al Fresco

Fava Bean Crostini, page 55
Vinho Verde

Niçoise Salad with Grilled Tuna, page 101
Côtes de Provence Rosé

Grilled New York Steak and
Summer Vegetables, page 145
Chilean Cabernet Sauvignon

Panna Cotta with Fresh Mango, page 159
Late-Harvest Gewürztraminer

Bistro-Style Supper

Savory Cheesecake, page 115
Cru Beaujolais

Tossed green salad

Herb-crusted Lamb Chops with
Celery Root Gratin, page 149
Crozes-Hermitage Syrah

Tarte Tatin
Sauternes or Barsac

Sparkling Wine Flight

Bacon & Onion Tart, page 71
Sparkling Vouvray

Smoked Chicken Salad, page 45
Pacific Northwest Sparkling Wine

Pappardelle with Spicy Lamb Ragù, page 129
California Blanc de Noirs

Wine-Poached Pears, page 160
Moscato d'Asti

Elegant Company Meal

Parmesan-Hazelnut Coins, page 42
Nonvintage Brut Champagne

Lobster Risotto, page 89
Pouilly Fuissé

Pan-Roasted Duck Breast with
Dried Cherry Sauce, page 135
Sonoma Pinot Noir

Warm Chocolate Cakes with
Raspberry Sauce, page 165
Ruby Port

Wine and cheese

Traditional thinking suggests that bold reds are the best wines to pair with cheese, but while they pair well with hard, aged cheeses such as Parmesan, the best, all-around wine to pair with a variety of cheeses is an off-dry soft white, such as Vouvray, whose subtle flavors won't overwhelm the cheese. Sweet wines pair well with strong, blue-veined cheese, as their sweetness and acidity contrast with the cheese's salty, pungent flavors. For more on pairing wine and cheese, turn to page 33.

Glossary

Acidity: Also called tartness, acidity is an important natural component of grapes that helps the wine achieve balance and structure. A wine with too much acidity tastes unpleasantly sharp; a wine with too little acidity tastes dull and flat.

Appellation: Used generally, appellation refers to a delimited and geographically defined wine-growing region.

Aroma: The smell of a young wine, or of the grapes used to make the wine. Often used as a synonym for bouquet.

Aromatic: A tasting term that describes wines, usually white wines, that have perfumed or spicy aromas.

Aromatic elements: The flavor perceptions in a wine that are perceived by the olfactory system.

Auslese: A classification category for German wine made from grapes picked after the regular harvest, which have a higher sugar level.

Balance: A wine is in balance when all the elements, including acidity, tannins, alcohol, sweetness (if any) and oak (if any) come together in harmony.

Barrel aged: Refers to wines that have been aged in small oak barrels following fermentation for varied periods of time. Barrel aging adds softness and richness to a wine, and also imparts oak flavors and tannins.

Beerenauslese: A German wine category that is applied to wines from individually selected, overripe grapes, leading to rich, concentrated dessert wines.

Bitterness: Astringent elements that help give dimension to wine and food. In wine, bitterness comes from grape skins and oak barrels. In food, bitterness comes from naturally occurring compounds in such things as artichokes, leafy greens, and cruciferous vegetables, as well as from some cooking methods like grilling.

Blanc: French word for white, as in *vin blanc,* or white wine.

Blush: A term invented in California as a marketing strategy for slightly sweet rosés, such as White Zinfandel.

Body: Also called mouthfeel, a wine's body refers to the feeling of substance it forms in the mouth and is described in terms of weight, fullness, or texture.

Bold Reds: A style of red wines that share the common traits of full body, strong flavors, and high tannins.

Botrytis cinerea: See Noble Rot.

Bouquet: The smell of a mature wine, reflecting the changes in a wine as it ages. Often used as a synonym for aroma.

Breathe: A word used to describe the process of exposing wine to air to soften its flavors and tannins and expand its bouquet before drinking.

Brut: The most popular style of Champagne and other sparkling wines, Brut refers to a wine that has less than 1.5 percent added sugar and tastes dry in the mouth.

Buttery: A tasting term that refers to a flavor perception of butter in the wine, commonly associated with New World Chardonnays.

Champagne method: A lengthy, labor-intensive process in which a secondary fermentation takes place in the bottle in which the wine is sold to create complexity and trap carbon dioxide. It was invented in the Champagne region of France, and is now used worldwide in the crafting of quality sparkling wines. Also called *méthode champenoise.*

Chewing: A tasting term that refers to swishing the wine around thoroughly to all parts of the mouth in order to gain a full impression of the wine on the palate.

Chewy: A tasting term often used to describe highly tannic wines.

Citric acid: One of the acids in wine, particularly noticeable in whites, that gives wines a flavor like that of lemons.

Classico: An Italian word signifying the historical center or a region, usually where the best wines of that region are produced.

Cold fermentation: A type of stainless-steel fermentation that occurs under carefully controlled temperatures to preserve a wine's freshness and acidity.

Complement, complementing: A wine-and-food-pairing concept that is based on bringing together items with similarities in their aromatic, flavor, and/or textural elements.

Complex: A tasting term that refers to a very good, balanced wine with distinctive layers of aromas and flavors.

Contrast, contrasting: A wine-and-food-pairing concept that is based on bringing together items with distinct differences in their aromatic, flavor, and/or textural elements.

Cork: The bark of a type of oak tree, cork is the traditional closure for wine bottles. Cork producers and wineries are researching alternative bottle closures to eliminate the problem of cork taint (see below).

Corked: A descriptive term for wine that has been affected by cork taint, caused by a mold in cork bark that gives the wine an off flavor. Cork taint affects about five percent of all wines that are sealed with a cork closure.

Côte: French for hillside or slope, a favored position for vines.

Crianza: A Spanish term relating to the aging of wine. On a label, *crianza* refers to the youngest oak-aged category of wine. *Sin crianza* denotes a young, fruity wine with little or no oak aging.

Crisp Whites: A style of white wines that share the common traits of high acidity, light body, and little or no oak flavors.

Cru: The French word for a particular piece of land or vineyard. Sometimes used in reference to a larger area or vineyard, as in Beaujolais.

Cru Bourgeois: French Bordeaux classification, which ranks just below the 1855 classification. Wines vary a great deal in quality, but can be a very good value.

Cru Classé: Refers mainly to the 1855 Classed Growths of Bordeaux, but also to other wines from official classifications in France.

Crushing: The first step, after picking, in winemaking, during which the grape skins are crushed to expose the juice, giving the yeast easier access to the sugars to start fermentation.

Decanting, decanter: The process of pouring a wine from a bottle into a glass vessel, called a decanter, used to either remove sediment from an old wine or to aerate a young wine.

Dry: A dry wine refers to a wine that is the opposite of sweet, or a wine with less than 0.5 percent residual sugar.

Earthy: A tasting term that refers to the smell of earth or soil present in a wine.

Fermenting, fermentation: The process by which yeast converts the sugar in grape juice into alcohol.

Finish: A tasting term that refers to the length of time a wine's aftertaste lingers on the tongue.

Floral: A tasting term that refers to the aroma of flowers in a wine, usually a white wine.

Flute: A narrow wineglass best used for Champagne and sparkling wine, as it does not allow the bubbles to escape too quickly.

Fortified wines: Certain wines that have had alcoholic spirits added to increase alcoholic content, or to stop fermentation while some grape sugars remain in the wine.

Fresh: A tasting term for youthful, simple wines.

Garnacha: The Spanish name for Grenache.

Grand cru: The French term for great growth, reserved for the best vineyard sites in Alsace, Burgundy, Champagne, and parts of Bordeaux.

Grass, grassy: A tasting term that refers to an herbaceous aroma in a wine.

Green: A tasting term for wines that have clean, grassy or herbal flavors, often attributed to young white wines.

Halbtrocken: A German word meaning half dry, an off-dry wine style between the dry trocken wines and sweeter wines.

Jammy: A tasting term that refers to rich, concentrated fruit flavors, often applied to California Zinfandel and Australian Shiraz.

Juicy Reds: A style of red wines that share the common traits of high acidity, light body, and little or no oak flavors.

Kabinett: Refers to German wines with the lowest ranking on the governmentally controlled ripeness scale.

Late harvest: A wine in which the grapes are picked several days, even weeks, after the normal harvest is finished. The wine is sweeter due to the buildup of sugar in the grapes. Fermentation is stopped before all the sugar is converted to alcohol.

Lees: Consisting mainly of dead yeast cells, lees are the sediment that settles to the bottom of barrels or tanks following fermentation. Wines left in contact with the lees develop complexity and additional flavor.

Legs: The tracks left on the inside of the glass by some wines, which are caused by the alcohol in the wine; also called tears.

Malic acid: One of the acids in wine, particularly noticeable in whites, that gives wine a flavor like that of apples.

Malolactic fermentation: A secondary fermentation, following the basic alcoholic fermentation, which converts harsher malic acid to milder lactic acid.

Maturing, maturation: The process of aging a wine in a tank or barrel, which takes place after fermentation and before bottling. During this time a wine will soften and develop complexity. A wine might go through another period of maturation after bottling.

Méthode champenoise: See Champagne method.

Minerals, minerally: Tasting terms that refer to an aroma reminiscent of stones, chalk, or mineral-laced soil in a wine, usually a white wine, often thought to be the taste of a wine's terroir.

Moelleux: A French word meaning mellow, referring to a slightly sweet wine.

Monastrell: The Spanish name for Mourvèdre.

Mousseux: The French word for sparkling, often found on wine labels from the Loire.

Négociant: French word for a merchant who buys finished wine for sale. Some négociants add finishing touches to the wine, including aging in barrels and/or bottles before selling.

New World: Refers to the wine-producing countries that do not belong to the Old World, including North America, South America, Australia, New Zealand, and South Africa. It can also refer to ways of growing grapes that rely more on technology than tradition. New-World wines are generally marked by up-front flavor and fruitiness.

Noble rot: The English term for *botrytis cinerea*, a fungus that attacks ripe white wine grapes and, if the weather conditions are right, dries them out, resulting in intensely concentrated sweet grapes.

Nouveau: The French word for new, referring to a style of wine intended to be consumed within weeks of its production.

Oak: The top wood choice for storing and aging wine, oak lends flavor and complexity to a variety of wines, both white and red. New oak barrels impart wood tannins to wines, while older oak barrels add softness and complexity.

Off dry: A tasting term that refers to a wine with between 0.5 and 3 percent residual sugar, or a wine that tastes slightly sweet.

Oily: A tasting term that refers to a rounded, viscous feeling on the palate, commonly found in oak-aged Chardonnays.

Old clones, old vines: Grapevines of a certain age that, in theory, produce more concentrated grapes. There is currently no legal definition for old vines in the U.S.

Old World: Refers to the European countries where wine grapes were first widely planted. It can also refer to ways of growing grapes that rely more on tradition than technology. Old-World wines are typically heavily associated with the place from which they originate.

Pink Wines: Also called rosés, this style of wine is made from red grapes that are left in contact with the grape skins for a short amount of time to achieve a fresh flavor and pink hue.

Premier cru: A quality level just below *Grand cru* in French wines.

Pressing: The process of separating grape juice from grapes using pressure.

Punt: The indentation in the bottom of a wine bottle, originally designed as an area for sediment to collect.

Reserva, gran reserva: Spanish and Portuguese words for wines of above-average quality that meet certain aging requirements.

Residual sugar: The total amount of sugar remaining in a wine after fermentation, expressed as a percentage of grams per liter.

Rich: A tasting term for a wine with great depth of fruit and a powerful, long finish.

Rich Whites: A style of dry white wines that share the common traits of full flavor, full body, and often influences of oak.

Rosado: The Spanish word for rosé.

Rosato: The Italian word for rosé.

Rouge: The French word for red, as in *vin rouge*, or red wine.

Saignée: French for "bled," *saignée* describes a method of making rosé in which the juice of red grapes is removed, or bled, from the fermenting tank after very brief contact with the grape skins, and then fermented separately to make light, refreshing pink wine.

Saltiness: Saltiness in food comes from natural salt (like in fish or shellfish) or added salt and the level of saltiness can have a profound effect on the wine match.

Sediment: The solid substance left after fermentation, consisting of dead yeast cells, bits of stem, and seeds.

Smooth Reds: A style of red wines that share the common traits of medium body, velvety mouthfeel, and balanced aromatic, taste, and tactile elements.

Soft Whites: A style of dry or off-dry white wines that share the common traits of honeyed or perfumed aromas, medium body, and little or no oak flavors.

Sparkling Wines: A style of wines that share an effervescent quality.

Spiciness: In wine, spiciness refers to the impression of a spice like pepper or anise, which is perceived through the nose as an aromatic element. In food, spiciness usually refers to the "hot" sensation imparted by chile peppers. The level of spiciness in a dish can have a profound effect on the wine match.

Stainless steel: Refers to the material of the tanks used for fermenting and aging a wine to preserve its crisp, bright flavors and a light body.

Structure: The structure of a wine is the sum of the relationship among all of the wine's elements—acidity, tannin, alcohol, sugar (if present), and oak (if present).

Super-Tuscans: Wines made in the Tuscan region of Italy from all or part non-native or nontraditional grapes.

Sweet: A sweet wine refers to a wine that is the opposite of dry, or a wine with more than 3 percent residual sugar.

Sweetness: A natural component of grapes that gives a wine balance and dimension. Food can also have a measure of natural sweetness.

Sweet Wines: A style of wines that share the common trait of a high amount of residual sugar. Some sweet wines are fortified.

Tactile elements: Also called texture, these are the perceptions in wine and food that are related to the sensation of touch.

Tannin: An astringent substance that comes from both grape skins and oak barrels. Tannin causes a dry, puckery sensation in the mouth, akin to sipping a cup of overbrewed black tea. A wine with high amounts of this substance is described as tannic.

Tartaric acid: A key acid in wine, which lends a fresh, tart flavor to the wine.

Tartrate crystals: Crystalline deposits that can form in wine after fermentation, caused by deposits of tartaric acid salts.

Taste elements: Flavor perceptions in wine and food that can only be perceived by the mouth, including sweetness, sourness (acidity), bitterness, spiciness, and saltiness.

Tears: See Legs.

Terroir: The influence that every aspect of a vineyard site, including the soil, sun exposure, wind direction, vineyard microclimate, and other natural elements has on the wine when it is brought together with the human element. It is also referred to as a wine's sense of place.

Toasty: A tasting term that refers to a toasted, nutty, smoky aroma in a wine, which comes from aging in oak.

Trocken: The German word for "dry."

Trockenbeerenauslese: A German word translating as "dried berry selected," meaning that the grapes in a sweet wine have been affected by noble rot.

Tulip glass: A glass shaped like a tulip with an opening that tapers inward, which aids swirling and tasting a wine to appreciate its array of aromas and flavors.

Varietal: The grape variety from which a wine is made.

Vieilles vignes: The French term for old vines. In some areas, the term old vines refers to vines that are more than 20 years old, while in other areas the term is used to describe vines that are over 50 years old.

Vin gris: A very pale rosé style made by pressing red-skinned grapes.

Vintage: The year in which a wine was harvested, and/or the wine was made.

Worm: The wire spiral on a corkscrew that is twisted into a cork to extract it.

Yeast: One-celled organisms that are responsible for converting the grape sugars into alcohol.

Yeasty: A tasting term that refers to an aroma of bread or bread dough, common in many sparkling wines and some still whites.

Wine Index

General Index

WILLIAMS-SONOMA

Founder & Vice-Chairman Chuck Williams

GOLD STREET PRESS
AN IMPRINT OF WELDON OWEN INC.

Chief Executive Officer Weldon Owen Group John Owen

President and Chief Executive Officer Weldon Owen Inc. Terry Newell

Chief Financial Officer Simon Fraser

Vice President International Sales Stuart Laurence

Vice President Sales & New Business Development Amy Kaneko

Vice President & Creative Director Gaye Allen

Vice President & Publisher Hannah Rahill

Executive Editor Jennifer Newens

Associate Editor Juli Vendzules

Assistant Editor Julia Humes

Art Director Marisa Kwek

Production Director Chris Hemesath

Color Manager Teri Bell

Production Manager Michelle Duggan

WILLIAMS-SONOMA WINE & FOOD

Conceived and produced by Weldon Owen Inc.
814 Montgomery Street, San Francisco, CA 94133
Telephone: 415 291 0100 Fax: 415 291 8841

In collaboration with Williams-Sonoma, Inc.
3250 Van Ness Avenue, San Francisco, CA 94109

A WELDON OWEN PRODUCTION

Copyright © 2007 by Weldon Owen Inc. and Williams-Sonoma Inc.

All rights reserved, including the right of reproduction in whole
or in part in any form.

Set in Griffith Gothic

Color separations by Embassy Graphics, Winnipeg
Printed and bound in China by Midas Printing Limited

First printed in 2007.

10 9 8 7 6 5 4 3 2 1

Library of Congress Cataloging-in-Publication data is available.

ISBN-13: 978-1-74089-622-1
ISBN-10: 1-74089-622-X

ACKNOWLEDGMENTS

Weldon Owen wishes to thank the following people for their generous support in producing this book

Designer: Marianne Mitten, Mitten Design; Photographers: Jeff Tucker and Kevin Hossler;
Recipe Authors: Coleen and Bob Simmons; Food Stylist: Kevin Crafts;
Assistant Food Stylist: Alexa Hyman; Consulting Editor: Sharon Silva;
Proofreader: Kate Washington; Indexer: Ken DellaPenta;
Photoshop Imaging: Justine Corey-Whitehead, Lightbox Productions

Eberle Winery; Joh. Jos. Christoffel Erben; Lauren Hancock; Alex Joerger;
Jeff Morgan; Julia Nelson; Leigh Nöe; Palm Bay Imports, Inc.; Kyrie Panton;
Domaine Jacques Prieur; Rodrigo de los Rios; Frederick Wildman and Sons, LTD

Additional photo credits

Adobe stock photos: pages 5, 7, 95, 109, 123, 139, 153; Avis Mandel Pictures: pages 8–9, 12–13, 14;
Getty images: truffles, pages 140, 143; Adrian Lander, page 6; Jason Lowe: page 4, 35, 49, 65, 79